DEMONS
&
DELIVERANCE
IS IT FOR TODAY?

Dr. Janelle Wade

DEDICATION

This book was written for those who desire information or have a need to have a better understanding of the spirit realm in approaching demonic spiritual warfare. I do not pretend to have all the answers; however, my hope is to give insight to Biblical knowledge and understanding of the ministry of casting out demons.

Contact Information for Dr. Wade:

Just Believe Ministries
PO Box 264
New Haven, IN 46774
(260)414-6356

ACKNOWLEDGMENTS

In appreciation, I would like to thank the following people who helped in making this book possible. First, my loving husband, Kirk, who has always stood with me with his ever present show of love, encouragement, and faith in the call of God on my life. Thanks to our secretary, Shelley; to our Assistant, Linda; and our daughter-in-law, Sandra, for all their time and help in the production of this book. To all our ministry partners who have been so faithful to Just Believe Ministries and Kirk and me. You have made this all possible. Thank you. Most importantly, I thank God for His love and for bringing people into my life who were aware of my personal need of deliverance.

DEMONS & DELIVERANCE: IS IT FOR TODAY?

Many people think that deliverance is not for today. People think that it was for when the church started, in the New Testament, but that we no longer participate in casting out demons. I want to challenge you to open your mind and spirit to some truth in the Word and by some personal encounters that we as a ministry have encountered. Keeping in mind, **Mark 16:17**. Here, Jesus tells us "And these signs will follow those who believe; in My name they will cast out demons."

The first place you will find Satan as being real is in the Garden of Eden, in **Genesis 3**, where he beguiled Eve. He came in the form of a serpent. He is called a serpent there, so people say, "Is that Lucifer?" I believe it was Satan in the form of a serpent. He is the one who is the head of sin. He is the one who brought it to Earth. I believe it is him. It is said in **Genesis 3:14** that the serpents had legs before this, but because of the curse placed on the serpent, they no longer have legs and must crawl in the dust forever because of what happened with Eve. That is the first time we really see that there is an evil thing on planet earth. At that time, everything was beautiful and wonderful in the Garden of Eden. There was no sin. Today, we cannot even fathom what it would be like living in a place where there was no sin.

Lucifer came in the form of a serpent. He was on Earth. When he caused man and woman to sin, it was the beginning of sin falling on mankind. In **James 2:19 (b)** The devils believe and tremble, so I don't know why Christians don't believe!

Jesus came to Earth because of sin. In Job, there are many chapters and verses on Satan. **Job 1:6-10** There was a time in Heaven when the sons of God came to God and talked. God conversed with Satan. It calls him Satan there. Satan asked Him, "What about your servant, Job? You have a hedge of protection around him." God said, "I will take it down. You can do whatever else, but you cannot kill him." Satan conversed with God about Job. That was a real being that was conversing with God. God knew him. Satan had no purpose but to do terrible evil to Job, the man of God. Read about Job, and you will see the things Satan did to Job, but he did not kill him. With Job, we see that there is a real entity.

We also remember **Daniel 10:12-13**. When Daniel prayed, the angel said, "Then he said to me, Do not fear, Daniel, for from the first day that you set your heart to understand, and to humble yourself before your God, your words where heard; and I have come because of your words. But; the prince of kingdom of Persia withstood me twenty-one days; and behold, Michael, one of the chief princes, came to help me, for I had been left alone there with the king of Persia." That proves that there is spiritual wickedness in high places, as well as war in the heavenlies. We are sitting here, and we are all safe. But there is spiritual wickedness in high places in this world, and they are called demons and devils. They are out there and on assignment against the church. They already have the world. They are winning that assignment, but there is an assignment against the children of God.

Why should we cast out demons, as the Holy Spirit directs us to do so when we encounter them? Jesus Himself did this on multiple occasions. It was one of the reasons that so many people followed Him wherever He went, once He began His ministry. They were looking for physical healings and also for the deliverance from demons that they had heard about from others or seen with their own eyes, as He ministered to those who had been plagued with demons for years. Consider the following scriptures as evidence of Jesus' desire to set the captives free. According to **Mark 3:14-15**, He also gave that same authority to His disciples, and therefore, to us today.

Mark 1:26 And when the unclean spirit had convulsed him and cried out with a loud voice, he came out of him.

Mark 1:32-34 Now at evening, when the sun had set, they brought to Him all who were sick and those who were demon-possessed. And the whole city was gathered together at the door. Then He healed many who were sick with various diseases, and cast out many demons, and He did not allow the demons to speak, because they knew Him.

Mark 1:39 And He was preaching in their synagogues throughout all Galilee, and casting out demons.

Mark 3:9-11 And He told His disciples that a small boat should be kept ready for Him because of the multitude, lest they should crush Him. For He healed many, so that as many as had afflictions pressed about Him to touch Him. And the unclean spirits, whenever they saw Him, fell down before Him and cried out saying, "You are the Son of God."

Mark 3:14-15 Then He appointed twelve, that they might be with Him and that He might send them out to preach, and to have power to heal sicknesses and to cast out demons.

Mark 3:22-23 And the scribes who came down from Jerusalem said, "He has Beelzebub," and, "By the ruler of the demons He casts out demons." So He called them to Him and said to them in parables: "How can Satan cast out Satan?"

Mark 5:9 Then He asked him, "What is your name?" And he answered, saying "My name is Legion; for we are many."

Mark 5:12-13 And all the demons begged Him, saying send us to the swine that we may enter them." And at once Jesus gave them permission. Then the unclean spirits went out and entered the swine (there were about two thousand); and the herd ran violently down the steep place into the sea, and drowned in the sea.

Question: Where did the demons go?

Answer: They are spirits, so they never died. They are part of the demonic warriors still here on Earth today.

When I was born, my mother dedicated me to the Lord, Jesus Christ. I grew up and I did (as many of you have) all these things wrong. Sin, sin, sin, sin. You think Satan didn't remember when I was dedicated to Jesus? The minute we dedicate our children to Jesus, the enemy is after them. He doesn't want them to grow up and be his enemy. He is after them even at an early age.

Kirk and I had a counseling ministry in our office and home on the east coast after we were married. We found that many of the people that called us to take their children through deliverance, the children had Biblical names. You had Matthew, Mark, Isaac, Isaiah, Sarah. The minute you name your child a Biblical name, the devil hates them. You know why? Because it's the Word, and he hates the Word.

Matthew 12:27 "If I by Beelzebub cast out devils, by whom do your children cast them out? Therefore, they shall be your judges." Jesus was telling them Satan could not cast out himself.

Matthew 12:28 "But if I cast out devils by the Spirit of God, then the kingdom of God has come unto you." The fact that Jesus cast out devils and demons, and He is telling us that the kingdom of God is coming to us, He is starting to tell us that we are going to do the same thing He is doing. I don't know why we are afraid to do it, but it seems that ministry today does not handle that part of ministry. They used to call our offices and some people still do, for us to take people through deliverance. These would be Spirit-filled, on-fire, men and women of God that would call us (pastors, psychologists, therapists), looking for someone to do the job that all of us should be able to do because of Who is in us. We can do this because of Jesus Christ -- not because of our flesh.

Matthew 17:19 Then came the disciples to Jesus apart and said, "Why could we not cast him out?" They had come across a demon that was so big in this person, that when they tried to cast him out, he would not come out. They asked Jesus, "What are we doing wrong?" It's not that the demon is bigger than other demons. It's because we have to position ourselves to be stronger than that demon. Many times we are walking in the flesh, and many times we have fear. Many times we are not walking with God like we should. We are not full of the Word or prayer.

We are not full of praise. That demon has certain powers that try to stop us. That's what Jesus said. He told them, "Go fast and pray and it will come out." He told them, "These don't come out but by much fasting and prayer."

Today, people are getting back into the real fasting time. There was a time when the church didn't fast anymore. If they did, they would say, "I'll give up breakfast. I'll give up lunch. I'll give up Pepsi." Much fasting and prayer is when you do without food. I never work with a team of people (I usually use five people) without first telling them to fast for three days. Don't eat anything, read the Word, and pray in the Spirit. Then I know that we come into unity. About the time you have someone that did something wrong, and go in to cast out a demon, guess what happens? The demons will start telling on them. They will say, "I know what you watched on TV". And it throws the whole team into confusion. And the demon will try to take the authority away from you. We need to get back into fasting and prayer like we never have. Why? You say, "I don't even see people possessed. I don't even know what you're talking about." You know why we probably don't see it? God loves us so much that He doesn't let us see it, because He knows that we aren't ready for it. He doesn't want us hurt. He is going to get us ready for it, because I honestly believe that Jesus Christ is coming. Before He comes, I believe that we are going to see people by the 10s and 20s at a time, come in from the streets full of alcoholism, drug addiction, adultery, pornography, and doors that have been open in them allowing demons to come into their bodies and minds. We are going to have to cast them out. We have to get ourselves ready for that, and we can't cast them out if we are having problems with sin ourselves. God is trying to clean us up. Fasting and prayer doesn't make you stronger than the devil, but it makes you clean enough to go in and kick him out.Many times, in Matthew, we will find scriptures where Jesus will cast out mute demons or deaf demons. He will cast it out, and they can hear or speak again. With epilepsy, sometimes they cast out a demon and other times, they were just healed. Whenever you are praying for somebody and they have a sickness, you have to pray for discernment. You must have the gifts of the Spirit functioning in you that are spoken of in **Galatians 5:22-23.** The only way the gifts are going to have the right power to do what we need them to do is that you begin to harvest the fruit of the Spirit. If you don't love somebody, don't go up and try to cast a demon out of them. I don't care what you are discerning. I don't care how much truth you walk in. If you can't walk in love, then you better watch out. When you go in the Name of Jesus, that means in the character of Jesus Christ. In the character of Jesus Christ gets the job done. Many people come in His Name, but not all of them belong to Him. We have to get ourselves to the place that we are the Name of Jesus. We have to get ourselves to the place where when the devil sees us coming, he runs--not us! We see that **in Mark 1:38-39**, Jesus said to them, "Let us go into the next towns that I may preach there also, because for this purpose I have come forth. And He was preaching in their synagogues throughout all Galilee and casting out demons." When I read that, it jumped out at me that it said, "in their synagogues." That was their churches back then. Something is going on in the church. You ask me, "Can Christians be possessed?" Derek Prince says no. Lester Sumrall said absolutely not. But I also read some articles before the end of their lives, where they said that they know something happens. I don't know if they can be possessed, but I know they can be oppressed. They can also be demonized when there is a place in the person that the demons can hang onto where they won't let go of a sin problem, a habit, or an attitude. Are they possessed? No, but it will flare up repeatedly. I have seen the times that I have cast demons out of or away from people like that, and they have had total victory and still do. Are people in the church possessed? They can be, but we must make sure they are not demonized. You know why they are? I believe this. When I pray for people at the altars, I pray for them and they receive Jesus as their Savior, or maybe I pray for healing. I whisper in their ear, and I bind up any demonic stronghold and cast it out of their flesh in the Name of Jesus. Once in a while, you will get one that will start burping and throwing up, or even start foaming at the mouth. Most of the time, that person never has any clue what you have done. What is wrong with us? Why is it so fearful to cast it out? In our flesh, we can have problems and our spirit will be okay. But our flesh will end up ruining our spirit if we don't get rid of some of these things. I will constantly pray those words to bind up any demonic strongholds so that I know when they walk out the door they are going to be okay.

We have to be careful in the church. We can't go around finding demons in everyone in the place. I have seen churches that have done that, and it tears the whole place up. You can have a problem with a demon and not be possessed by that demon. You can be doing things right, and it is trying to do things wrong in your life. Don't look at people saying, "I bet that's a demon". Stop that! We should be ready, and discern it. The house of the Lord has failed in discernment. We need to be asking God for that gift all of the time so we can discern things and discern people. I can walk anywhere, in a store, in a church preaching, and discernment kicks in and I will know exactly what is wrong in everybody's life. I will even see their sin. I remember an Aglow meeting down in Virginia. I prayed for a lady who went down in the Spirit. God told me she had a lesbian spirit. She was married, but had a lesbian spirit that had never totally let go of her. I got down in her ear, and I bound that lesbian spirit up in the Name of Jesus. She started crying, not from sorrow, but glad it was leaving her. That thing left her, and afterwards she came to me crying and hugging me, saying, "That thing has plagued me since college. I don't do it and don't want it, but it has been a problem." She had gotten saved, but she didn't get delivered until that time. Once somebody recognized that (but you must be careful – discernment!), she could be set free.

When you start talking about demons, people walk up and blurt things out. God wants us to have the fruit of the Spirit and the rest of the gifts functioning. You can have truth, but if you don't have wisdom to know what to do with it, you can destroy a person.

We have power to heal sicknesses and cast out devils. In **Mark 3:14**, He appointed twelve that they might be with him, and that he might send them out to preach and to have power to heal sicknesses and to cast out demons. I am telling you that demons have got to be real. Hollywood believes in them more than the church. They make movies about them all the time. When I was a young lady in a church, I was youth director in a church that was not Spirit-filled. The pastor took us in a place to eat. We went in to eat, and I sat down. I told the pastor, "I can't eat, Pastor! I can't eat with demons!" There were posters of gremlins on the wall. I was fresh enough out of the occult and what I had seen with my own eyes to know they were fashioned after something that humans don't see too often. There are a lot of things coming out of Hollywood that they fashion after the very looks of demons. Somebody is seeing demons in Hollywood. They are making us believe that they are little Smurfettes, or good demons/bad demons, good witches/bad witches. They have poisoned our minds to the truth. We are desensitized in our thinking about the spirit realm. We have to get back to being sensitive enough to know what is going on. Jesus told us they were real. He says in Matthew, "Satan, I saw you fall like lightning to the earth." Lucifer was in Heaven.

Ezekiel 28. Many scholars believe that this (King of Tyre) is about Lucifer while he was still in Heaven. It is a description of who he was. Verses 12-15: "Son of man, take up a lamentation for the King of Tyre and say to him, thus says the Lord God: You were the seal of perfection, full of wisdom and perfect in beauty. You were in Eden, the garden of God. Every precious stone was your covering: sardis, topaz and diamond, beryl, onyx and jasper, sapphire, turquoise and emerald with gold. The workmanship of your timbrels and pipes was prepared for you on the day you were created. You were the anointed cherubim with covers. I established you. You were on the holy mountain of God. You walked back and forth in the midst of fiery stones. You were perfect in your ways from the day you were created, until iniquity was found in you." He was in Heaven!

I look at people today and say, "What have you let in the doorway of your home?" I take them to this scripture and tell them, it is satanic music. Don't let it in your home. It attracts demonic powers. The devil (Lucifer when he was in Heaven) took the praise. He was full of musical instruments of praise, items of praise to God. When he came to Earth, what did he want? What got him out of Heaven? Jealousy and pride. He wanted to be like God. He came to Earth and said, "I'll set up my own kingdom. I'll make my kingdom just like it is in Heaven." He wants praise. God got praise, and that is what the devil wants. He had to create that for himself, and it is through music. I am telling you that if you go into some of these places where they sell clothing for young people, you can hardly stand to be in there because of the music that is being played there. In some of the restaurants, you can hardly eat for the evil music that is being played there. Do you ever feel it closing in on you, and you can't wait to get out? That's because it is not of God, it is praising the devil. Many of the singers and musicians way back (we used to study back-masking) would say that the stage is their pulpit and the audience is their congregation. The kids go around making this sign (the sign of the horned god --- Satan). When they all come together, they are in unity at these concerts. That is the reason why the evil gets so bad, because they come into unity more than the church does. I can't stress unity enough. You don't have to like each other very well. You don't have to always agree. But we can be in unity and love if we want to. The enemy cannot cross the line of unity, because he knows unity is Blood-bought through Jesus. He doesn't know what love is anymore, and he can't cross it. That's why he doesn't want us to walk in it, because it has more power than he has. When he gets in unity, he gets power when anyone will agree with him. When he came to Earth, he set up a social order. I know these things because I know where I was. I know what the witches study, and I know what Satanism does. I know what they believe and I know their social order. I know what their social order is. Lucifer is all power. Underneath him are princes. I was taught that princes do not enter bodies. They get worship from covens and groups of people. Have you heard of spontaneous combustion? They are so powerful, if they came inside a body, it would burn it up. Under princes are devils. The Bible talks about devils. The devils, you will find, mostly mess with the head. People that are in mental institutions, people that are having problems mentally, they are dealing with devils. They are mean. They are all mean, but devils will mess with the mind. Demons get no respect in the order. They get no worship except from people, from flesh. So they want in us, and they want to find a way in. We can open a door and let them in if we are not careful. I'm not talking about Christians, but we're talking about out in the world, we can let them in and not even know we opened the door. Then there are these little things called unclean spirits. They hang onto people, and people don't recognize them because they say, "I've been this way all my life." Even little things like smoking cigarettes can be an unclean spirit. I said, "Can be." Any kind of bad habit can be just an unclean spirit. It is easy to cast out, but it's only easy if the right person comes into agreement with you. There is a whole social order on planet Earth. They are to glorify evil. They are working and intellectual. I can't believe

Christians don't believe the devil is smart. He is highly intellectual. He was in Heaven with God. He knows the Word. What did the devil himself tempt Jesus with? He tempted Jesus with the Word. Jesus would look back and say, "It is Written." He was reminding the devil not to even try to fake him out. He was saying, "You know the Word." If you are going to defeat the devil in your life, or anyone else, you better be able to say, "It is written". The Spirit wants to move through us, but He only moves on the Word of God. He honors the Word of God.

Sometimes we have to realize that God answers prayer, but He answers it on His time. We can forget that we have some problems ourselves that God is working with us on. Just sin bugs us. It is not demons; it is just our natural flesh. It is hard to discern sometimes what is demonic and what is just sin, or flesh rising up in our life. I have had people come to me and ask me to cast something out. I look at them and say, "I can't cast out sin. You have to repent that out." If someone keeps committing adultery over and over, and are truly repentant and hate it, you might want to look for a demonic power there. Again, you must have discernment. You can tell why they call Satan the angel of light. He is so brilliant with all those jewels. He will put on his shiny cloak sometimes. He isn't going to let you know he is there. We have lots of ministers, Christians, teachers, and singers that have that beautiful cloak on, but if you remove it, it isn't God at all. It's an angel of light. When they fall, you want to fall. Many people do. An angel of light has been fooling them.

I was down in Virginia at a church, when we lived in our bus. We were on 12 acres of land out in the country, a beautiful place. I saw our cat out after some bunnies. I jumped off the bus to tell the cat not to get the bunnies. There was a pile of asphalt on the ground, and I didn't see it. I hit that, and it knocked me clear out of my shoes. I fell down on my hand and knee. I felt something push my head down violently twice. They had to call an ambulance. When I got to the hospital, they thought I was a lady that just hit an embankment in her car. In that fall, I had two fractures, stitches in my head, black eyes, my knees and legs were all cut up. I'm telling you this because there was an enemy there. I don't care who said it, there is no way I fell that hard and twice my head bounced off that asphalt. I don't know why it was allowed or what was going on. We had a lot of deliverances in that church, a lot of healings, some salvations, and we have been there many times. Sometimes the devil gets mad at us, and we are not protecting ourselves because we forget he's there. There are powers in the heavenlies that make war on you and me. We are more than conquerors, but we have to see that they are there.

I think of that little girl that followed Paul, in **Acts 16:16** who was saying "Here is Paul. Here come the disciples." He finally got so aggravated that he cast the spirit of divination out of her. My stepsister came to church one time where I was preaching. God told me she had a spirit of divination. He told me that if she came to the altar I should cast that thing out, and He would save her from it. You have to know my stepsister. She had a temper! She would give you a tongue lashing if you said something she didn't like! I was begging God for her not to come to the altar, yet knowing she would. She did. She knelt down with her hand on her head, getting nowhere in prayer. I asked her what was going on. She said, "I just don't think God is going to forgive me." I looked at her and said, "Do you trust me, Sis?" She said, "Yes, I do." I said, "Are you willing for me to pray what God told me to pray for you?" She said,

"What do I have to lose? Do it." I bound up the spirit of divination and cast that thing out. When I did, her head went back and hit the communion table. She was shouting and falling. She was totally set free to live for the Lord. I had to be obedient to God. I was really afraid, not of the demon, but in the flesh.

Sometimes people just get on your nerves. God may be showing you something in the spirit to pray in tongues over them. Maybe not in their face, but ask God to show you what it is. Sometimes I can go in a store, and can't wait to get away from some people. When I was in the grocery store once, a well-dressed woman was standing there, and I heard a voice saying, "I know who you are. You better not come near me." I thought, "What in the world?" She was getting her vegetables. Her lips were moving and she didn't even know it. God didn't tell me to do anything to her. I didn't. You better make sure God is telling you to do it.

Children today are being exposed to these demons, and they are having fun with them in cartoons, movies, video games, and many other avenues of access to their minds. The demons today are coming in the most beautiful bodies you ever want to see. The

Bible tells us that in the end days, we will be seekers of pleasure more than seekers of God. Watch commercials. I want to get on Nutri-System so bad. I just know if I did, I would look just like Marie Osmond. We are all being bombarded to be these beautiful creatures on the outside, but looking like the devil on the inside. How can you tell a child when they look at a gorgeous guy or girl that they are not of God? When I was growing up, you didn't even go around homosexuals. Kids today think everybody is equal, they are good people, they are wonderful people, everybody is okay. They bought me a candy bar, so they are nice. If they have a beautiful voice, they can't be bad. If they can play the guitar, they can't be bad. They are just looking on the outside of everything and are being taught that anybody can go to Heaven any way, through any god, or no god at all, and there's no hell at all. They are buying into it because they don't want to have to say, "If I sin, I am going to have to pay for it, unless I give it to Jesus." That is a demonic outpouring on planet Earth right now. It concerns me for my children and their children. If you tell the parents you can help their children, they will say no to you, then lead them down that road of destruction they know they don't want them to go down themselves. They know better for themselves, but are not stopping it.

You think Jesus isn't coming soon? He is coming. He has to. It just can't go on like this. Churches will believe in salvation and healing, but won't believe in raising the dead and casting out demons.

The full gospel of Jesus Christ came alive in the 60s and 70s. They were raising the dead, casting out demons, getting people filled with the Holy Spirit, churches were growing, and new churches springing up everywhere. Why? Somebody believed. What happened to the full gospel movement? Why don't they dance or clap anymore? Why are they sitting there dead? They are sitting there going to sleep in religion, and they are supposed to be filled with the Spirit, but they will say, "Don't make a noise, don't shout, and don't do anything that will embarrass our church. Let's keep it all in order." I have been told what to speak, how long to go, when to stop, how to pray for people, and how not to prophesy. Some of you travel too, and you get that sometimes also, I am certain. Some of leadership will tell you exactly what to do. They won't let God tell you. They trust themselves more than they trust God. We must stop that if we are full gospel. If we are filled with the Spirit of

God and we do it wrong, we should be able to take correction and next time, try to fix that problem. But we have to stop not letting God move. I would rather have a move of God any day of the week than go out for Sunday dinner at McDonalds or somewhere. I can go all day without eating if I can see God move all afternoon. I have had pastors come to the altar and drag me away from praying for people and ministering to them. After two or three or four, when there are 100 up there, they say, "You have done enough, come on." Your heart is just grieving as they pull you out. But, when you go into somebody else's house, it is their house and you better be respectful of it. If you are not, you will have to answer. I don't have to answer to God if they didn't let me minister, but I have to answer to them because it's their house and they know what they want to do with their house. They will have to answer to God for that.

We have to let God back in His church. We can knock a lot of churches out there and say they aren't letting God move, but how seeker friendly are we? We want to be accepted. We want people to like us. You want to know how I know that? I'm telling on Janelle. When I started out, I was a wild woman. Not bad wild. I didn't get weird. There were people in my life saying all kinds of things, but I didn't buy into it. I was strange because I still believed in demonic powers, and I believed in angels. I was so innocent and naïve about it. I thought everybody believed just like me. I remember going out of a prayer meeting in my home at about three or four in the morning. Two people were leaving, and I saw hordes of angels flying. I said, "Aww." I wasn't going to tell them. One of them said, "I know you saw something." I said, "I see angels". They both looked up and said they didn't see anything. Suddenly, one of them started seeing them. Then the other person saw them. I said, "They are just going to take care of our prayers." I saw them all the time. They would come around my bed and cover me with their wings. I saw them!

I have sat in a car with a friend. We put our hands together because the enemy was trying to tear us apart. We were declaring unity, and our hands disappeared in a cloud. I stopped all that. I can remember a time when I put my hand up, and someone said my hand just disappeared. I would take it down, then put it back up and it would disappear. People that I looked up to and ministered to made fun of me and mocked me and told me no one would let me come to their church if I talked about that. So I stopped all that. I had to repent. I'm telling you now that I do care what people think about me; however, I care more about how God wants to use me. It is His call on my life.

I saw a lady at an Aglow. She came through the line. As she got closer to me, her makeup began to run down her face as she was crying. Black just streaked her face. By the time she got to me, she had a horrible, demonic presence on her face. The women started backing off quickly, and so did a couple of men. They knew something was wrong with her. I told her friend, "I'm not going to pray for her right now. Tell her to make an appointment with me." There were too many people in that line needing prayer. Sometimes you can't pray for that person at that time, because they will take all the anointing and time, and they will rob everyone else who would have gotten a touch from God.

I came back home and I got my five people ready. I got Pastor John, who is built like a Viking. I got another man named Mike, who was built like a Viking also. They fasted and prayed too. When she came in, I told them to hold onto her, because I didn't know how bad off she was. I didn't want to get sued if she got hurt, so I wanted to make sure she didn't jump or roll around, levitate or injure herself. She lifted those two men like they were paper weights or just nothing. She was lifting them off the floor, bouncing them around the room. She didn't get hurt, but she got delivered. It took us 10 hours. People say you should be able to bind it, cast it out, and it leaves, just like that. I have much experience in this area. Sometimes, it takes time. Sometimes you are dealing with a demon, and sometimes you are dealing with the person. Ten hours later, she walked out of that room a free woman in the Name of Jesus Christ, and she still is.

She called me a few weeks later and said, "I'm pregnant." My heart sank. I knew she was not pregnant, but I didn't tell her that. A few months later, she called me from the hospital and said, "I just lost the baby." She said, "Janelle, I don't know what to think. One of the nurses almost fainted. It was just a black blob when it came out, and it stunk so bad you couldn't stand it." I just dismissed it as sometimes miscarriages could be like that. I wasn't going to hurt her. I knew she passed something. I knew she was going to. She got delivered. She ended up pregnant and having a little girl later on. She weighed 1.5 pounds, and the doctors had said she would die. She lived. God is so good!

Another little girl we knew, her parents were Christians. We had a lady in town there who had a jewelry store and wanted to do something for the teens on Friday nights. My friend that had the meeting did not always walk in discernment. She prayed for her and she went out on the floor, started slithering like a snake and sticking her tongue out, hissing all around. My friend said, "Janelle, can you help me? What can we do?" I thought, "What did you touch her for? Why did you do this to this girl?" I knew it wasn't right. This woman took a cross and put it on her head, and it burnt her head. She started levitating. Her little brother, who was just full of the Holy Spirit, got mad at the devil for doing this to his sister. He jumped into the middle of it (he was 10 or 11), and said, "Satan, I bind you in the Name of Jesus! You are not going to do this to my sister!"

Demons went crazy. That little boy had authority over them. She couldn't move any more, but the demons would not leave. There was also a minister there. As he watched, he came over on all fours and got down in her face and said, "Oh, Baby, if I could take these demons for you, I would take them myself!" I screamed, "NO! Don't you say that!" I knew it was going off the wall wrong. I closed it down.

That night, the woman that owned that place had just had four new tires put on her car. When we walked out, one of the tires was flat. Another young couple was there with a brand new car. As they started out of the alleyway, they had no brake fluid, and they ran into the wall. Another couple had to drive about an hour away. In the middle of the night, his brand new car broke down on the highway. God rescued him. The man that had gotten down on all fours owned a security company. One of his guards who was on duty had a man wielding a knife and was going to stab him. Two guys in a pickup truck saw him in the alley and went over and rescued him. The man who had gotten down on all fours died within a few months. You have to know what you are doing. And be careful what you are doing.

A young woman who was an anorexic that we counseled for four years and prayed for her, got delivered. She was a Christian at the time, but she had demonic problems. She is now living a wonderful life of freedom in the Lord. Glory to God!

I was called to a college one day to speak and pray over the girls. Upon doing so, a young lady came to me and told me how she was a lesbian. I began to pray for her and saw by the Spirit a goat-like creature inside her total body standing up. She would come to my house, and I would talk to her for hours. A few weeks after I had gotten to know her, I had ministry in Virginia. She wanted me to take her new car and I did. I was driving through Kentucky, when suddenly I came out of a daze and realized I was lost on some back roads. The inside of the car started getting extremely hot, so I tried to roll down the windows. They would not budge, and I started to panic in fear. I finally found a place to stop and get directions and to cool off. When I got back into the vehicle, everything was fine again. I had tried to counsel and help this young woman, but she never wanted to be set free.

So many things were going on as God began to use me in deliverance. A friend and her family needed desperately to move from our hometown to Nevada, but for months and months could not get any hits on their home that was for sale. I went out to visit them one day, and the Lord spoke to me to tell them that "land binding spirits" would not let go of their property. I had never heard anything like that in my life. I wrestled with it, but finally told them what I felt. They were to walk their property line, anoint it and break the hold of these land binding spirits. I thought they would think me crazy, but they trusted the power of God in me and did it. The house sold immediately, and they were packed up and heading for Nevada two weeks later.

After marrying Kirk, I moved to Virginia. At that time, a ministry found out about us and asked us to be their east coast deliverance ministry that they could direct people to. We accepted. Some months we would get many calls every day for help. I had such a heart for the hurting people that I just said yes to everyone. It was a great training time for Kirk and me, as well as others who would help us. Most ministers did not want any part of helping us, so I had to depend on Holy Spirit and His gifting in helping those in need. Kirk had never seen demons nor people possessed before, so he just backed me up and believed in what he experienced, watching God work through me and those helping me. He would always fast and pray with me. I didn't want this as part of our ministry, but felt like someone had to do it. I would be so hurt at the way ministers especially would act toward me. I was just doing what the Word had commissioned all of us to do. I admit I did not understand why they didn't want to be a part of the miracle of seeing lives change in a moment of deliverance. I fully understand now. I was on the cutting edge of the ministry of recognizing demonic activity.

A minister in another state brought me his wife for us to help. She ended up having multiple personalities. She had been ritually abused as a little girl. She would receive much deliverance and help during her visits to our office. She will always be a special love in my heart.

A pastor from Richmond, VA brought a lady and her children to us. They had all been ritually abused. We were blessed that they were placed in a safe house. She was delivered and helped, and they went on to serve a productive life and got away from the coven.

We had a young woman brought to us through a ministry contact. She was a card carrying witch that had not yet gone through her initiation. When we first dealt with her, she would hide a large open safety pin in her hand and clasp it in her fist to cause her pain as she hid in the closets. I was able to recognize it, and we pried it out of her hand.

She was doing it on demand of the demons, to remind her to keep silent. She would punish herself for talking to us, which at first was very little. She ended up staying in our home for several years. Much counseling was required, and I found her to have a stubborn streak in her personality that would hide in silence. We did all we knew to do to help her, but then we had to let her go. Sometimes she was against us and held secrets. She was a definite satanic ritual abuse victim with multiple personality disorders. Through another ministry, many of the stories she told us were investigated by professionals and were proven true. Even the people that did it were called out by name, as well as the different locations in different states. They all existed and lived as well as worked in the cities and places she named, during the years she spoke of. It was even proven that she had lived in an orphanage, and was taken by those who were supposed to be in ministry to a dungeon where they did all of the rituals. She did not want to press charges. She would have had to have proof, which was gone after all the years. She had surgery when she was staying with us, and I will never forget how she looked when she came out of recovery. Her eyes were scaled over and she kept saying

"I am sorry." For what I could not fully understand and does not need to be told. The nurse informed me that they had a terrible time keeping her knocked out during surgery. I knew it was the multiples taking over from one to another. I loved her like a daughter, but it was evident that I needed to let her go, for all our sakes. The last I heard, she is doing well and going to a church in a big city. I pray for every blessing in her life. She was used terribly in the occult as a child, and it may take her the rest of her life to be made whole. If she stays with Jesus, she will have the hope she needs. I know she needed more help in the natural than I knew how to give her. You must know how far you can go or take someone else. Multiple personalities are more psychological, as they are spiritual. I am not trained in that field, so I am smart enough to do what I can and then let go and let the right people take over.

We had a young man sent to us from a well-known Christian clinic. He was a warlock. He stayed with us three and one-half months. We took him to our team at another home, and he took off running out the basement door. I made everyone stay in and not go after him. It was a very cold fall night and I was not in the mood to run after the devil in him. I asked the Holy Spirit to send angels to bring him back. I knew he was in a strange city and could be lost, but I just wasn't going to concern myself, as I just knew he would be back. Sure enough, sometime later two of my team motioned he was at the door. I had already became aware of him and told them to leave him alone and not go outside where he was. They did not listen to me and opened the door. The man was almost naked where he had torn his clothes off and was wielding a two by four. He was ready to hurt them if they proceeded. You must listen to the leader. I went into action immediately and commanded the demons to bring his body back into the room. His eyes were like fish eyes, and he was drooling and barely human. At the Name of Jesus, he was forced to respond. He came into the house and sat down on the floor Indian-style and took a glob of slimy stuff from his mouth and swathed it on the floor, encircling himself. His hands went up, making the satanic sign as he dropped his head and shifted his eyes upon me. I stood there watching and praying doing my best to discern the situation and hear from God. Two of the team attempted a couple of things, and he reached out of his circle attempting to get violent with them. He hit their leg. That instantly angered me to the point that I reached down with my oil-filled hand and swathed through the ring he had made and I made a cross as I said, "I give you a way out, in the Name of Jesus." He screamed, cursed, and his face distorted, but he started to get victory, or at least we had the power flowing in the Name of Jesus. We had to laugh as odd as it sounds. The two people that he touched their leg each had a prosthesis, so he never really touched them. As he sat there in his circle, he would take his spit and make a satanic sign over his heart, and I recognized the sign and would rebuke him. He seemed to get some deliverance, so we headed to our home where he would stay. We took him with us wherever we went for the next three and one-half months. During one of our many sessions with this man, when casting out demons, a spider came out of his mouth. It was red, had no hair on it, and it was transparent. It fell down on a towel on his lap. When you are seeing these things sometimes, you have to keep a sense of humor. I looked at my husband and said, "I don't do spiders and snakes!" Kirk took care of that one!

Weeks later, he would have his wife he was separated from bring their three-year-old son to us from out of state. We took them to our dad's church and sat him on the altar to pray for him and break every spell over him. His father had told us that he had taken him to a coven meeting and had him dedicated to Satan. As we began to pray for the little boy, he began to manifest and went into a trance-like condition. We had his mother pull his shirt up and anointed his heart area, at his father's insistence. We watched as the boy, murmuring, took his hand and began to draw the same satanic sign over his heart that his father had done weeks prior in that room. Then he began to cry and scream and we knew he was back with us and we stopped immediately as not to damage him any further.

This young man, we would find out later, was in our area to do nothing but cause separation and division in churches and people. Once when he was posing as being suddenly blind, we had his former pastor and wife come down to see him. I knew he was not blind, and that it was a demonic ploy on the goodness of Christians who would be deceived by him. His former pastor was coming off a forty-day fast and this man was no match for the power of God in this pastor. I watched as he took his Bible and told this young man to read it. He started his act and squirmed trying not to, but this pastor commanded him and after a short moment, he began to read the Bible. I was thrilled to see this great man of God expose the ploy of the enemy. I would like to tell you he ended up well, but he would leave the area and go back to his own way. He never reunited with his wife and two children. There is more to this story, but I have written enough about him. He would be totally blind for days then he would see again. He would go to the altar at the Pentecostal church he went to, go to the altar and fight the anointing. I knew what he was doing. If he could go and not give into the anointing it would give him, so to speak, brownie points in the spirit realm.

On one occasion, a lady brought her friend who was having such problems with demonic power that her body had become squared in shape. She brought a picture of herself two years prior to this time, and she had a gorgeous figure, was beautiful, had beautiful eyes, and was just a striking young woman. Here she is, square-looking, one eye went one way, and the other one went the other way. Every time we started praying for her, she would shake her head and spew blood at us. We kept praying and trying to help her. She would not get delivered. At the very end of it, she ended up admitting she did not want to be delivered. You know why? She said, "It's the way I get attention and people show me love!" When you get them to this place, you have to let them go. You cannot go against their will.

A girl who was into occult activities was brought to us by her grandmother. The grandmother wanted us to help her understand how dangerous witchcraft was, and to get her out of it. While praying for her, I saw by the Spirit, a troll doll at the bottom of her bed and up on a shelf. I asked her what I was seeing. She and her grandmother's eyes widened as she told me that she did have one that was given to her by another person in the group. I told her she would have to get rid of it, as they often give an object that they attach a guardian spirit to that has the legal ground to come into your home through. I then saw a creature that was like a dragon. She then told me that she had an iguana as a pet. She had gotten it, so I felt it was okay for her to keep it as long as her Christian grandmother anointed it. She did what I asked and as far as we ever knew, she was victorious.

A man was sent to us from Maryland and we took him to the home where we had our team come in to help with his deliverance. He was very nice and had become a Christian, but something was wrong yet in his life. He was aware that it was demonic. I knew we would have victory, as he was a willing vessel. We pulled out a huge antique trunk for him to sit on so we could all get around him. As we began to pray for him, at one point his tongue came out and was as long as a cow's tongue, and went back into his body. A few minutes later, the trunk crashed to pieces beneath him, but he was still delivered!

After Kirk and I were ministering in a church in another state, the altars were filled and we were praying for all manner of needs. The pastor's wife was in line with their little girl about five years old. She was their adopted daughter who they adored, but she was having problems. It was evident that she did not like me, nor would she have eye contact with me. Her mother asked me to pray and cast anything out that she might have carried with her. I began to bind up every ancestral spirit and told them that their assignment was broken and cast them out. When you are dealing with children, you don't yell and scream, as you will scare them. The child would not look at me and she squirmed under my hand that was on her head. They left and later her mother would tell me that when they got into the vehicle to leave, that they had not gone too far when she suddenly and violently threw up all in the back seat. Her attitude and actions changed immediately. She started loving me.

Many times, especially years ago, when we would be going into a church for several meetings, they would advertise me as a former witch. That in itself would attract certain people. Those who were in paganism and witchcraft would often show up. We were at this church when we noticed that the back row on our side filled up with what we would later know as pagans. I was told before the meeting that some church members were bringing in a male witch with them. They came in and took the front row of seats across from us. At the aisle seat was a young man who I knew was being used as a guardian for the warlock on the other side of the row. Now I do not play games, but inside a chuckle came up in me as I heard the Spirit say, "Before you minister, have the church family love on all the visitors." Being obedient, I did just that. I headed straight to the warlock. He absolutely didn't know what to do, but let me hug him. He was all in black with a long black coat, with his hair dyed black. I asked him to stay after the meeting to talk to me, and he agreed to. At the altar call, the first person to come up and receive Jesus was the one who was supposed to be his guardian.

After the altar service, I headed straight for the warlock and sat down by him. His pants had pockets on the side of them and I tapped one and said, "Is that your book of shadows?" He was shocked and said, "How did you know?" I looked at him and laughed as I told him that he has to take it with him wherever he goes. He took it out. We had a great visit about where he was and where I had been, and he said he would come back.

The next five nights, he would only miss one service. As he sat there as I preached, every night he would shudder and squirm in his seat to the point of disfiguration. As I preached, I would ask God in my spirit if I could go cast the demons out, and He would not let me. By the end of these services, I had found out from him that his grandmother was a Christian who always prayed for him. I told him that he may as well give up, as now I was in agreement with her. I would never see him again. About two years later, the pastor's wife asked me if I knew what happened to him and I said, "No." She began to tell me how this young man had eventually gone to another city to join a larger coven, but God intervened and he got saved and was studying for the ministry. "Yes!" I shouted.

One Christian young man who we met had been in a family that practiced witchcraft when he was a child, and had been involved in many Native American rituals. He had fangs for teeth. He kept asking God to take them away, and one morning he looked in the mirror and his teeth were normal. We have a BIG God.

In a very small town in the mountains where we ministered on many occasions, we encountered a situation where the church we were to minister in and the pastor and his wife were being almost stalked by a priestess that had come in from California. We prayed a lot, as we did not want to get into emotions or fantasize it. In getting to know this person better, it was evident over the next months that she was sent to destroy their work. Thank God for my friend, the pastor's wife, as she has sound discernment and wisdom, and is a powerful prayer warrior. Many demonic things were trying to be done, but none were accomplished. Thanks be to God. Naturally, this woman tried to get close to me, and I knew her tricks all too well. I would never allow her access to deceiving me. She would even follow me to other churches, bringing us either monetary gifts or objects worth money, trying to smoke screen us into thinking she was innocent. The pastor's wife tried to help her in every way possible. We were once again in the area, and she was telling us that she had gone to a large city and was having the tattoo of the pentagram and 666 taken off of her head. That was why she was wearing a fake piece of hair in the back. I sat her down in a chair and asked her to take the piece off, and she did. On the back of her head was a fresh tattoo of a pentagram, crown with a sword through it dripping blood and the number 666. It was so fresh that it still had scabs and bright new colors to it. I had looked in her hair before and saw none of this. I looked at her and fire came up in me as I told her to leave. I actually said, "You lying devil, get out of here now." The pastor's wife was in total agreement with me. After that time, she attended less and less. The last time I heard, she was incarcerated.

Across from that same pastor's church was a huge two-story brick building that housed some people who were believed to be in the occult. They would make certain remarks to and about the church that they were trying to place curses on, so we kept reversing them.

One day their building caught on fire and burnt to the ground. No one was hurt, but the funny thing about it is that our pastor friend's church building needed a new roof and windows. It was a huge three-story building. During the fire, the sparks from the building that was burning damaged the church's roof and caused the windows fire damage, so the insurance (of the people in the building that burned) had to pay for the church repairs. Not only that, but the land that their building was on became the parking lot for the church. A small structure that was attached to the back of the church was owned by some other people who were thought to be into the occult also. The church wanted it, and the lady told them that she would sell it to them for a huge price, so they never bought it. They just continued praying. After a while, she came to them and said the city was going to charge her the same amount of money she had asked for the sale price of it, and that would be just to tear it down, as it had become a public hazard. She said she could not sell it to the church, but she would sell it to the pastor's wife for a dollar. She bought it, and they tore it down and sold the bricks for the same amount she had held them hostage with. How big is our God?

We were ministering in one city where we encountered a warlock who had been sent to take over the city and was certainly on an assignment against a pastor and his family. She and another woman had a store together. The warlock was this woman's brother from another state. He could hardly stand me. Many odd things happened during this time, like his washing machine ran over and he got so mad, as it was supposed to have happened to the pastor's washer. It seemed like many things that he would come against these pastors with would come back on him. Don't think for one minute that demonic spirits won't try to take you out or have a plan against you. Just remember who you are and who is in you. Their power becomes null and void at the Blood and Name of Jesus. This young man wanted to go back to his home state, but couldn't and I know why. He failed his assignment, thanks to Jesus and His warriors.

One of the most memorable times while there was when I was at the store and we were anointing the furniture and things without anyone knowing what was going on. When we finished, I had been aware that this lady was sitting in a chair at the counter and I spoke to her. She said, "I know what you are doing." I said, "What?" She said, "You are anointing everything," and then she held out her hands and asked me for the power. She looked at me as if in a daze and said, "Please give me your power." I knew she was part of a coven, and I did not want her hurt, so I told her the consequences if I did. I told her that if she had me do this and continued with the coven, that she would most likely die. She said she knew that, but still wanted the power. I debated inside myself trying to hear the voice and will of God. She asked again and I placed my hands on her hands and prayed for her and covered her with the Blood of Jesus. She squirmed and shook as I prayed. I told her to please get into a Bible-believing church, for her sake.

Several months later, my friend would call me and tell me that this woman had died, and by the time her family returned home, they could not find one picture of her or the books she wrote in. Someone had come in and taken it all. She kept the books for the coven she was involved in. This broke my heart, but I knew that I knew that God wanted to give her a chance.

I'm sharing with you not to scare you, but to let you know that greater is He that is in us than he that is in the world; however, you must have a trained team to work with that will follow instructions. There can only be one leader, not that the other team members can't help, but they go through the leader to do what they feel the Holy Spirit is leading them to do. He is going to restore us. The enemy is beating people up. He has beaten our children up, and our grandchildren. We have to get our minds back on Jesus Christ and realize that we have authority, but we don't have anything if we don't take it. We have to take back what the enemy has stolen. I am tired of seeing it. I am a warring woman of God right now. I want to see God do some great and mighty things.

We must begin to realize that truly there is a spirit realm all around us, and in it are beings good and evil. When we get saved, we no longer belong to the natural realm, but we begin to live in the supernatural. We begin to realize eternity is where we will live forever. We have to begin to get out of our natural man into our spiritual man and begin to war for our loved ones. We are not alone. We have angels that war for us and with us. **Hebrews 1:14** "Are they not all ministering spirits sent forth to minister for those who will inherit salvation?"

Psalms 91:11 "For he will command His

angels concerning you to guard you in all your ways."

RECOGNIZING DEMONIC ACTIVITY

We want to recognize demonic activity, but in doing so, we have to look in the right place, through the right eyes. In recognizing demonic activity, you will have to open up your spirit, and you need the Holy Spirit to show you in discernment as you walk in this world.

II Corinthians10:3-6 "For though we walk in the flesh, we do not war according to the flesh, for the weapons of our warfare are not carnal, but mighty in God for pulling down strongholds, casting down arguments and every high thing that exalts itself against the knowledge of God, bringing every thought into captivity to the obedience of Christ."

We see that inwardly, we need to explore and make sure there are no demonic strongholds within us or from the outside tormenting us or causing us problems in the mind and flesh. Here we see we have the power in us to bring down those strongholds. We can cast down those arguments. These scriptures are telling us we have the authority to take authority over our own minds, and also over our own thoughts and deeds. This is one place of inward battling that we have to do ourselves. We have to be careful when we do it, because sometimes we are not dealing inwardly, but we are dealing outwardly.

Ephesians 6:10 "Finally, brethren, be strong in the Lord and in the power of His might."

If there is ever a scripture that is powerful for us, that is one! We are trying to be strong in ourselves. We must understand this is not our war. It is His, in us and through us. We are not alone. We must be strong in the power of HIS might**. Corinthians 6:11-12** "Put on the whole armor of God that you may be able to stand against the wiles of the devil. For we wrestle not against flesh and blood, but against principalities, against powers, against the rulers of the darkness of this age, against spiritual hosts of wickedness in heavenly places." This is an outward show of warfare. There is an inward show, and now there is an outward show. When you go to an outward show, outside your body, you better make sure you listen to **Ephesians 6** and get your armor on. You shouldn't be fighting against yourself. You should be submitting yourself to the Word and Spirit of God. He says we can't think certain things, we can't argue, we can't fight, we can't hate one another. We can't have envy or jealousy or strife, and most of all, we must walk in forgiveness. Sometimes demonic powers from the outside can cause an inside war zone that we have to conquer. You can't use armor against yourself. You can only repent. Repentance and the Word is one of the greatest armaments we have to be victorious against things the enemy throws at us about ourselves.

When you put on the whole armor of God, you will be able to fight against heavenly things in dark places. This world looks light right now in the natural, but if you could see this earth through the eyes of God, there is a horrible darkness of sin and degradation upon the earth. That is the darkness where these things hang out. They live in the darkness of the atmosphere, so to speak. Many years ago, by vision, I was taken up far above the earth and seemed to be looking at the earth through the eyes of God. He bid me to look and see, as I peered at the earth, I saw what looked like a covering of dark beings moving all over the face of the earth like swarms. I knew it was the demonic powers of hell that had been unleashed upon the earth. As I peered through the darkness I saw Europe and it was dark, but throughout it, I would see twinkles of light and one or two large beams of light. All throughout so many of the European countries as well as Asia, it was mostly dark with the same pattern of twinkle and once in very few areas a large beam would shine through. Then He bid me to look at Africa and the Middle East and it was mostly darkness with only a very few small lights coming forth until you looked down the coastline of South Africa and it seemed to be pretty well lit up. I did not know what the meaning of what I was seeing meant, but I watched. Suddenly the earth turned and I was totally blinded by the light from North and South America. I asked what I was seeing and the Lord told me that the light was representing the believers praying and praising Him. At the end of that vision, I then and still to this day can only assume what the world will be like when we are all gone. In **Ephesians 6:14** "gird your waist up with the truth." The truth is part of your armament. Don't leave it behind. That's what I'm saying when I say, **John 8:32** "The truth will make you free." It will hurt you making you free. I never got freedom from things without hurting, because I had to learn the truth about Janelle. That's when you go back to **Corinthians 10:3-6**, and you begin to fight the fight in your mind. You have to submit the mind and pull down those strongholds.

You can't get in arguments over the truth. If it's in the Bible, it's the Word, and you better live by it or you won't live at all as a victorious Christian. Put on the breastplate of righteousness – that is not your own! When I see people walking around with their own little breastplate of righteousness, thinking they are victorious – in themselves (building themselves up), I know that they have no idea that Jesus and His righteousness is meek and lowly and humble. We must make sure that our righteousness is in Him, not in ourselves and what we know. **Proverbs 16:18** "Pride goes before destruction and a haughty spirit before a fall." Self righteousness is pride.

Ephesians 6:15 "…and having shod your feet with the preparation of the gospel of peace…"

But you may not always have peace. Don't think you are in sin because you are not in peace. We are to be making preparation for this. When someone does something against us and then comes back and repents, we are to be prepared to forgive them there. That is the preparation we make. Paul talked about the gospel of peace. The Romans wore sandals with seven-inch spikes on the bottom of them. They would march down the street in those shoes that made a tremendous sound, and as they walked, anything in front of them would be mowed down. The gospel of peace digs into rocky places to keep peace. I haven't always wanted to walk in peace with everyone. I have to dig myself a place with these shoes of peace, and realize I am not fighting that person; I am fighting the enemy that is trying to get me out of unity with my brothers and sisters. I will dig in, and prepare to forgive when they come and ask for forgiveness.

Ephesians 6:16 Shield of faith: You quench the fiery darts with the shield of faith. Continually build your faith. You will never build your faith without the Word of God.

Ephesians 6:17 Helmet of salvation: If you set your helmet of salvation to the side to go out in sin, you have opened yourself up to every demonic power out there. You are still saved, but you took your armament off. There are fiery darts of the enemy waiting for you to take that helmet off. Your mind is your conscience and it can become blinded without a secure helmet to guard it.

Ephesians 6:17 The sword of the Spirit (Word of God): Christians, who never read the Word, never listen to it, never study it, don't know it. If you don't know it, you will get yourself in trouble. The Word was how

Jesus overcame the devil himself in the wilderness. "It is written." The Word has got to be written on your heart. The Word tells us that the demons know it and tremble, so often they will throw some scripture at you too, to try to hinder you from recognizing them for who they are. You might give pause to them and question if it is a demon or not. After all, they speak the Word.

Ephesians 6:18, "Praying always in the spirit, being watchful with perseverance". You have to have patience. Sometimes we don't know what is going on until God shows us. We must persevere until He shows us. Hold on and wait on the Lord.

I John 4:1 "Do not believe every spirit. Test every spirit whether it is of God, because many false prophets have gone out into the world." That spirit here in the Word represents the spirit of the person. We have to look at people and see what spirit they are coming to us in. We must ask ourselves, "Is that what God would do? Is that the Lord? Is this right?" We think that whenever we test spirits, we are testing demonic spirits. You are not. You are testing the spirits of people, whether they are of God or not. You must be careful and be wise. Pray for discernment!

The Word has never changed. We have. I

heard today on a Christian television program I was watching, that the call (prophet, teacher, apostle, etc.) in **Ephesians 4:11** is not a call, it is gifts, a description of what you are supposed to be doing for God. Many people take it as a call, and we need to be what that call is. We need to make sure of our position and walk in that. That is hard today, because many people say "the Word changed from back then – it was just for the beginning of the church, it's not for today". So the church has gotten to be a mess because we have had no prophet to correct us or change us or tell us where to go. We have had no apostle to tell us, "This isn't how it's supposed to be". They did away with the prophet and the apostle! So then we can't even test the spirits of man, let alone find out where a demonic spirit is. So we have to be careful. We have to get ourselves back into it. We have a lot of zealots out there, but that doesn't mean there are not a lot of good people out there.

I quit casting out demons and talking about demonic warfare and witchcraft years ago (and I had to repent of it in the last year and tell God to do with me whatever He wants), because I wanted to fit in. I didn't want to be different. I could recognize demonic powers. I can stand in a pulpit preaching and recognize sin in peoples' lives that they would faint if they knew I saw it. When I get out of the pulpit, I hardly ever remember anything, but while I'm there, I could terrify people with what I see in their lives. I don't want to see it, and I don't see it so I can go back later to tell on them. Jesus said, "I perceive their very thoughts".

In **Acts 19:14**, it talks about the seven sons of Sceva. They were casting out demons. The demons said, "I know Jesus, and Paul I know; but who are you?" The spirit jumped on them, in verse 16, and overpowered them and prevailed against them and they fled naked and wounded. Don't go in and cast anything out unless it's God. If God doesn't take you, don't do it. And when you do, make sure your heart is right with God before you go. God does have things that we are to do to keep the blessing flowing. People get hurt over things they are saying and doing because they were not prepared in prayer and fasting before they go. A demon has always known me when I walk in. Sometimes I have had people that were demon-possessed tell me, "I hate you" or they'll try to hang on me. When someone deals with possession or demonic powers in their life, they will try to put a shield up. They will try to get you either in confusion or say how wonderful you are – like Paul in **Acts 16** when the girl with the spirit of divination was saying, "Here they come, the men of God!" Paul finally had enough and cast the spirit out of her. She was saying all the right things. Paul discerned the spirit of divination. Divination can read palms, and give futuristic things. Nobody talks about this one. If somebody is going to have a baby and they don't want anyone to know, then you go and tell what shouldn't have been told in order to get the glory for knowing in advance, that can become a spirit of divination. It never keeps quiet, and it can never keep a secret. It wants to be the first to tell everything.

They will come to you and try to make you do like the devil does – appealing to your pride, bragging on you. They will give you money. Money talks big. How can you tell someone they are demonic when they are giving a $10,000 check, when no one is paying tithes in your church? Suddenly, that person will not be called out for the demonic activity. We see it all the time in ministry. I have seen great ministries call sin what it is -- sin. Then that person comes in with sin in them and gives them a big check, and then no longer will they call that thing sin. That is what you have to be careful about with divination and demons. They don't come in with horns, growling and hissing, tail out the back, and wearing red. The devil doesn't come in like that. He comes in often in sheep skin. Sometimes he comes in looking very beautiful. Very nicely dressed. That's when you say, "Surely not". In this world we live in, they come in wearing the finest of clothes, but many of them have demons inside their bodies. You must be careful of "I love you's". They will try to get into your pride area. We can all have pride areas. We want to be number one and notice we are okay. Some of us suffered from low self-worth. Somebody bragging on us can get our eyes off of God. They can give us smoke screens.

Before I met Kirk there was a man that came into my life. He was not for me. I got on my knees, screaming out and begging God to take this man away. I did not want to sin, and I knew he wasn't for me. I had been single 11 years, and I wanted somebody to love me. God literally took that man totally out of my life. I knew it was God that removed him. Just a few months later, I met Kirk. A smoke screen will always come. Pastors fight this all the time, people wanting them to okay being unequally yoked with someone. "Are they a Christian? Is this of God?" The people say, "No, but I just feel like they'll get saved!" No they won't! It's a smoke screen! You don't give yourself over to the enemy. You don't get with that person unless or until he/she turns to God! That's where you get in trouble, and they leave you about that time.

There are times while encountering the demonic when you may get dizzy. I'll feel something in a person – that's one of the first signs. When I get dizzy, I wonder what's going on, and it will try to get me off course. You may get dizzy or nauseous or feel sick or have a headache. It can affect your body. Your natural person can be affected when someone around you has a demon. Not everything is from a demon, but I'm saying be aware of those things. If you are with other Christians, you will have confirmation. Many times, if there is a demonic person around, Kirk and I have to be careful. We will start arguing, and suddenly realize there is no reason for it. Aha! We just passed somebody that was having a problem. Be aware of that. Pray, pray, pray for discernment!

Some people will tell you to get out or call you names to get your mind off of what is going on. Don't let them pull you off course.

This is usually during deliverance. Voices can change. Eyes can change. I have seen eyes go from brown to green, then a red look, or sometimes a white look. I begin to recognize past the natural. Look for those things.

James 3:13 "Who is wise and understanding among you? Let him show by good conduct that his works are done in the meekness of wisdom. But if you have bitter envy and self-seeking in your hearts, do not boast and lie against the truth. This wisdom does not descend from above, but is earthly, sensual and demonic. For where envy and self-seeking exist, confusion and every evil thing are there."

Many ministries and ministers are self-seeking. They don't want to talk about anyone else's ministry or their church or their evangelistic ministry. They are always building themselves up or name-dropping. I have been on Christian television on *TBN*, *700 Club*, spoken to major colleges, been all over the place, radio, magazines, etc. Not one of those things helped our ministry grow. People will advertise that I've "been on *TBN*" and it doesn't bring one more out to see us. But a move of the Holy Spirit will fill the church up! When we lift the Name of Jesus, the Holy Spirit will come right in there. I am not a self-seeking person, although ministry tried to get me there. I knew I wasn't going to sell a lot of books on my life story. I didn't want anybody owning me or this ministry. Through the years, I slipped and let things and people own me – not sin, but well-meaning things and sometimes ministry itself, dictated the move of God. I'm not there now. I'm not self-seeking. I'm seeking Jesus, and a real move of God, to let people exercise things and learn how it feels to feel a move of the Holy Spirit and stir up giftings in them. It's a place to let the Holy Spirit move like He wants to. Will somebody get off course? Of course, but we will bring them back in. We won't let them go. We are not self-seeking. We want a move of God.

Recognizing demonic activity: Look for people who party a lot, or are video gamers. I was in shock at the demons in the first video games I saw that nobody recognized. These were in Christian homes and in pastors' homes. I was shocked at how they just let it go. The kids are sometimes into Wicca, which is white witchcraft. They think there's nothing wrong because they don't take a blood sacrifice. They don't know it can lead them into deeper darkness of the occult. That's how I started.

Satanism and Wicca are religions. They all have tax write-offs as religious entities. The young people are turning toward it, and it does nothing but cause demonic activity in their life. My first encounter was in using a Ouija board. It was telling me things that I did not know for my future and they came to pass. I just thought it was coincidence. Demons are also very attached to pornography. Sexual sins are just passing around demonic powers from one person to another. Sexual acts that you do are supposed to be only between man and wife, because it's a covenant. Whenever you go out with different partners and perform sexual acts, you are making covenants with different partners and their demons, so you are making what is known as soul ties with them and often giving rights to transferring of spirits. People don't want to hear that, but it's the truth. These are called soul ties, and they can become familiar spirits. Not necessarily a demonic possession, but they can demonize your life and victory is harder to get to. You can break these strongholds of soul ties, but you must then stay away from the familiar spirits, such as, if you had addictions you stay away from those old friends or those you know are still bound.

Once in a while I'll go anoint the TV and say "God help me to not watch some things." You can't even watch some commercials. The other day, two commercials came on for kids, then right behind it a Victoria's Secret ad, then back to the cartoonish ads for kids. Look how subtly it's coming into our homes. It's soft porn, no matter what you think of it. You have to be careful. Demons attach themselves to our habits and our weaknesses. Sin begins in the heart: anger, bitterness, unforgiveness, jealousy, strife. Often people don't recognize these things as sin, but it is sin. If we quit smoking cigarettes, quit drinking alcohol, quit having premarital sex, quit going places we shouldn't go, and dress a little different, everyone thinks "They were saved, they are awesome". Nobody deals with the anger, bitterness, jealousy, strife, or hatefulness. They don't think that is sin too, I guess, but it is. Deal with sin in your life. Don't give the enemy a place to come in and say, "That's my place because it is sin and it belongs to me!"

Religious spirit: If someone has a prophetic word, people can get riled up and say that it is not a God word. I'm of the mind to say sometimes it is true, but not always. Denomination kind of sounds like demonization! Because it splits us apart and separates us, and that's what the enemy wants us to do. There are all kinds of churches and ministries out there that say, "If I don't get it, it can't be from God." It's not true. There are good people in every church. Denominations and churches are traditions of men. We must be careful. Some of those traditions are good and out of the Bible. Almost every denomination, if you go back in history, they will all say they spoke in tongues. People don't realize what they were founded on, and they've gotten so far away from all of it that they've taken the good stuff out of it – the move of the Holy Spirit-- and they've made it the traditions of man, not of God. They get so hypocritical, because they can't live it either. When they can't find anyone else to gripe at, they begin to eat each other. Nobody can be good enough except them, but they can only be good enough by making everybody else bad. That's not going to work. The only way any of us can go to Heaven is through Jesus Christ. It's alright to go to any church, but you better be going to a Bible-believing one, and you better go to a Blood-bought one and one that believes in the move of the Holy Spirit. In these last days, if we don't have Him to lead us, teach us and direct us, we will not make it. We must have the Holy Spirit.

I was thinking the other day about the parables that Jesus spoke in. We have too many people watching the people speaking in parables, and they are not speaking the Word of God. Pastors will preach a message and get Word out of the Bible, and they will get it in story form. Be careful that you may believe their parable and not the Word of God. You must be careful about the parables. Is that what it really means in the Word? Carry your Word with you to make certain what is being preached or spoken lines up with what the Word states.

In the Bible, Jesus cast out a blind and mute spirit, and in other places, He healed them. All sickness is not demonic. Sometimes they need to be healed. That's why we have the gift of healing. The body changes as you get older, but it doesn't mean you are doing anything wrong. At some point, the body will begin to age and need healing – not necessarily a demonic power.

In **Matthew 17:15,** it talks about the epileptic demon possession. This was a demonic spirit, and Jesus cast it out. Christians have some of these problems. Are they possessed? I don't know. Are they oppressed? They may be. Some are depressed. Depression can be a demon. Someone could have been raped at 5, 10, 12 years old or had a bad marriage or saw a murder, and today they have never gotten over it 25-50 years later. What you are seeing is they are still being raped, etc. in their mind because they are not bringing that stronghold down.

People want to know why I can live past my book, *Out of Darkness,* and my life. I tell them when Jesus saved me, behold I became a new creation. I read this in one of Kathryn Kuhlman's books, "If I live in all my yesterdays, I'll have no tomorrows". I thought, "The devil has robbed me enough. I'm going to have some tomorrows." God is in our tomorrows. Yesterdays are gone, so give them up. I will not let the devil rob me one more day with a tear or a cry or a scream. I had enough of that. I'm going to let God give me what He wanted to give me in the first place. You should too! We need to be healed in our minds.

One of my favorite teachings is on inner healing. We need people to know what that means. We need to get people healed. I believe Jesus is coming back for a glorious church, and I just pray He lets me be used in it just a little bit. Doctors are a good thing, but the thing we must be careful of is that we don't get to be pharmakeia Christians, dependent on drugs for everything. Sorcery, in the book of Revelation, is revealed as dependent on drugs. There is a gift of the working of miracles, and when we come into unity and agreement, loose our faith in the power of God, absolutely anything can and will happen. Sometimes my faith isn't real strong. I'm going to call somebody who has the victory that day. I'm not going to find somebody who is whining and weak like I am. I'm going to call somebody who has the victory that day to pray with me.

The only people that did not get healed were those that were full of doubt and unbelief. Those are the two big ones I have to fight all the time. How about you? I don't understand it. I'm not proud of it. I have to fast and pray to build myself up sometimes to get the job done. That's what it is about in deliverance ministry. You have to fast and pray. It isn't that the demon is bigger. It's because in fasting and praying you build up your most holy self, you get you out of the natural, and allow the supernatural of God to arise in you. It is then that you have the power to win the battle. Fasting and prayer is for us. Some answers I don't know. I'm glad I don't. I still need Jesus.

Dealing with recognizing demonic activity, I will often put my hand on their stomach, that is where the person's spirit is. If I do put my hand there, and they really begin to manifest, I begin to pray against demonic powers. I was in a meeting with someone from Papua New Guinea, and they said when they received Jesus, they receive him into their throat. That's where they think the center of there being is. Years later at a youth camp, one of the counselors sent someone to get me, as she had a teenage girl in the bathroom who she had been praying for. She said that she (being a novice in deliverance ministry) had tried to cast a demon out of the girl. When I entered the bathroom, the girl's throat was blown out like a frog and her eyes were rolled back in her head. I cast that thing out of her throat. Her throat went back to normal, her eyes rolled back down. She had no clue what had just happened and we felt it best to just assure her that she was fine, as we knew she had no memory of what had just transpired with her.

When I start touching a person, I can tell if they have problems. That is why I touch. With some people, I wait until God tells me to touch, and some people I don't touch because they don't want to be delivered. They just want to rob you of all the anointing. You must be careful.

People who are demon possessed or oppressed have killed themselves during sexual acts, or enjoy cutting themselves, because they hate themselves so badly. A young boy I picked up the other day told me he almost started cutting himself that day because it hurts so badly. He said, "I have this hole in me, and it hurts so bad." They are angry with themselves. He said, "It doesn't hurt as bad to cut myself as it does to think about that hole in me."

There are many young people cutting themselves, as well as being into vampirism. There is a lot of that going on in the world today. Kids are drinking blood. You think it doesn't exist? It is out there, and we must be aware of it. Sometimes they curse and scream at you when you begin to take authority. It doesn't matter about the strange things I hear or see, it just matters that people get set free. They are real. You can recognize it before you get to that point. You are in a war. You must know what to do. There are times you need to have much wisdom and discernment on what to do.

I was in one Women's Aglow in a certain city. They brought me a girl to pray for as I was praying for others. I realized that she would take all my attention from all the others that needed prayer, so I took two women I knew were prayer warriors and had them take her aside and pray in tongues over her until I could get to her. Again you must have discernment because they will zap the anointing from you. She was growling, hissing, speaking in a man's voice, foaming, doing it all. After a while, the whole scene changed behind me. I heard her start saying, "Thank you, Jesus!" They don't need you in order to have deliverance. They need Jesus! She was prayed through. We need each other.

Remember the woman **in Luke 13:12** who was bent over with the spirit of infirmity. Again, not all sickness is demonic, but this one was. She had a spirit of infirmity, and Jesus cast it out. Mary Magdalene had demons. Jesus said **in Mark 16: 17**, "And these signs will follow those who believe; In My name they will cast out demons; they will speak with new tongues." People don't do it, but we need to be aware. We want signs and wonders, but we want to not be mocked or have people afraid of us as a minister. Jesus cast them out in front of everyone, right on the streets. People followed Him with awe at His authority.

Something that controls our mental state is usually demonic. Depression or becoming withdrawn, hiding in secret places, can be a sign of demonic activity. A lot of kids end up in their rooms, lighting candles, have signs in their rooms, wanting to be in their rooms all the time, on their computers. They sometimes want things that are of darkness, like animals that are not clean for pets, such as scorpions or snakes. Their whole attitude will change.

One boy was beaten so bad by his mother, he hated her. She beat him so bad one day, from that moment forth, he started loving her--like worshipping her, and from that point on his grades went down to nothing, and he couldn't even read as an adult. She died a few years later, and he would hang out at the graveyard and talk to her and cry. I think a demonic spirit grabbed hold of him from her. His heart was broken, and he died of a heart attack as a young man.

A friend of my son's was a very handsome, talented young man. He would listen to his big boom box. He listened to awful heavy metal. He knew to come in my house, he had to set it down on the porch and turn it off or he couldn't come in with it. I saw him at 13-14 years old; the demons were racing to him. He had a bad home life. He would stay in my home for 15-20 minutes and begin to complain of a headache until he could listen to his heavy metal music again for about 30 minutes, so he would go outside. He worshipped Marilyn Monroe. He had noises and horrible things in his house. He had demons, but he would not let us do anything about it. We still believe God to deliver him. Demons will either go frantic or get very quiet when you come around. You must have DISCERNMENT.

A speaker and author, Howard Pittman, told of a time when he died, that the angel of the Lord took him to a bar. He said there were people around there with dark spirits sitting beside them. He watched the demonic powers moving around men, and the demons would reach for drinks and cigarettes and couldn't get them. When one man passed out, his aura split, and he saw bunches of demons go into his body and his friends carried him out the door and took him home.

I heard the singer, Jim Morrison, on a talk show once, and here is what happened to him at a young age. He was out with his parents on a road. A bunch of Native Americans had a wreck and died on that road, and Jim Morrison saw the spirits that were running all around as they left them. He felt sorry for them and told them they could come and live in him. Jim Morrison died at a very young age. Never invite them in – they will come!

There was a girl with Dr. Lester Sumrall. He went to an institution (she had seen her mother stab her father to death and kill herself). The little girl was completely demon-possessed. As Dr. Sumrall prayed, each physical attribute changed as each demon was cast out. She went on to live a normal life after the deliverance.

Demons can change form in a body. The body can twist up and get grotesque looking. You can have bite marks or bruises that you don't know how they got there. Things cannot be possessed (such as chairs, knives, and inanimate things), but a house can have spirits in it. An open space can trap a spirit. If they are sent on assignment to cities and to houses and they don't get the assignment done, they are cursed from the higher powers. Demons don't come into things – they will come into people or animals. I had houses that had demons in them. You could hear things screaming and yelling. One time after surgery, I came home and was sitting on a sofa that was directly under a vent that was upstairs. Nothing was up there – I had moved my kids out of the room. I still had staples in my stomach from a recent surgery and was not feeling very well. Suddenly, I heard something running across the floor above my head, and it jumped up on the bed that was in the room above and I could hear the springs from the mattress. It came over to the register and made horrible noises. I knew it was demonic. I ended up sneaking to the TV, crawled over the sofa, and woke the man up that was at that time my husband. He got his .22, thinking it was a coon or something. He went upstairs with me softly begging him not to and found nothing up there. Days later, we had someone come in and there was nothing there and no way to get in there. Later on he would tell me, "When we lived in that house, that's when I started to stop loving you." Something entered his body, and I know it. I saw it in him before he left me.

One other time, I was in bed (before I was saved) and the fan was blowing across the bed. My girlfriend called me on the phone and said, "Janelle, your fan is on fire! Get up!" I jabbed the man I was married to and said, "Get up! The fan is on fire!" I went back to sleep. The phone rang again. I picked it up, and she said, "Janelle! The fan is on fire! It's trying to burn you up!" I said, "OK!" I saw the flames coming over the bed. I said, "The fan is on fire!" He jumped out of bed. I still had the phone in my hand, but there was no one on the other end, I will always believe it to be a God call. He took the fan and threw it out the front door. We had purchased brand new smoke detectors in that house, one of which was right above the bed. Not one of them went off. We had the fire department come out and check the smoke detectors, and all of them worked perfectly. We gave the fan to a neighbor who had asked for it. He used it forever, and it never caught on fire again. The enemy is real. That is when I was in witchcraft wanting to get out so badly. That was not just a thing. It was something bad. Strange things will happen where demons are around.

Truly repent. Don't blame the demons. Just truly repent and God will see you through. Rebellion is the same as witchcraft, according to **I Sam 15:3**. The world is in a lot of witchcraft because there is so much anarchy and rebellion all over the place. Even people who claim to be Christians are in anarchy and against anyone being over them.

We need each other! Reba, my friend that went on to be with Jesus, told me, "Janelle, you need me! She said, "One chases 1000 to flight, two chases 10,000. What if there are 1,001 against you? You need me for that one!" It is truth. We need someone. Jesus sent everybody out by two. Remember that.

When you come across demonic activity, remember we have a force behind you! There is a time to be bold in this world, and there's a time to be meek. I heard a pastor say, "Don't take my meekness as weakness". Meekness is not weakness; it's just being Christ-like.

Gifts of the spirit are a must when you are in deliverance ministry. If you have a word of knowledge working, you better ask for the word of wisdom to know what to do with the knowledge. One of the ministers I know, when he gets a word, he will say, "I have to be careful". I love it when he does that, because he is discerning and using wisdom with it. He has a word from God, but sometimes he will say, "I can't give all of it yet". I look at him and think, "That man has got something going on good."

Demons will try to cause confusion. When our ministry team goes out, people will want you to pray with them over here and over there, to separate the team members. We must have backups. If they can get us separated, then that demonic problem will not be cared for because of confusion and not knowing what is going on. You have to be careful in connecting with the power of God, but you also have to flow in the Spirit of God to know what to do.

Don't worry about demons. They are afraid of you. They are going to try to make you be afraid of them. They have no authority over you. Luke 10:19 "Behold I give you the authority to trample on serpents and scorpions, and over all the power of the enemy, and nothing shall by any means hurt you." You are more than a conqueror through Jesus Christ who saved you. Don't worry about their threats. That's all they are unless you let them become more than that. Jesus Christ is the anointing that's in us. He is the Christ, the son of the Living God. We don't have a dead God, so when we have our force of life combined with the force of God Almighty through His Holy Spirit and the Blood of His Son, we are marked. Why wouldn't people know we are coming? We have a mark nobody can see right in the middle of our forehead, by the Holy Ghost. Those demons see that. We don't, but they do. We are powerful. We are mighty. We are awesome. You must see yourself as you are seen in the spirit realm and see your words as being His words.

II Timothy 1:7 "For God has not given us a spirit of fear, but of power and love and of a sound mind." Keep your sound mind. Keep a firm hold of Jesus Christ and the Blood. Remember you are Blood-bought by Him and are created by God, the Creator of all.

Here is a list of gates and legal ground that a demonic force can or may have entered into a person through. Of course the first would be ancestral spirits brought on through the blood line, incest and abuse as a child, sexual habits such as pornography as well as sexual sins, word curses by parents and people, even through being bullied by others, rape, seeing a murder or a horrific event, shut into closets or other confinements that leaves one abandoned to fear, occult activities, voodoo dolls made of a person to hold them in bondage in their spirit or body, games such as Ouija board, tarot cards, and all the video games that are violent or demonic, mind control or a controlling spirit, addictions of every kind, anger/rage, murder and any other emotions that are out of the normal realm of one's self controlling them.

Guardians will surface to keep you from

getting to the root of their problem. Those roots can be things like anger, sorrow, spirit of control, and the biggest is self-pity. They guard the gates and legal ground that the person has yielded to them (them meaning demonic forces). Whatever the need is to hide behind, the demons will use the very emotions and human weaknesses of the person possessed. I have found that you must stay aware that demonic forces can often be more than one in a person. They group, and you can cast out most and think you are done, as the person will change, but something is yet not right. Demons do what I call nesting. You have to get through the guardian demonic spirits to get to the big one, the one who is controlling the others and the person you are dealing with. So now you see, the person has emotional guardians and the demons have their own too. Just keep in mind that you will get the deliverance completed.

Again, when you come into the presence of a demon in a home or person that is manifesting, you will know. Sometimes your heart will begin to beat faster, or you will have a sense in your spirit that something is there. You will just know that. Sometimes I get really dizzy. I was recently in a church where the pastor has cancer. We were asked to come and speak there, and as I got in the pulpit, I got so dizzy that I didn't know where to go. I was confused. You will get into confusion with that dizziness. I stood there and began to weep because I didn't know what to do. I didn't want to tell the pastor that I felt a demonic spirit in his pulpit! I didn't do anything at that time, but I will get back to them on that. It could be what is attacking him. But at the end, a young man came forward and was delivered of demons, so it could have been that. Again, use discernment.

When you walk into a place, especially when you are Spirit-filled, there will be people around you that will react to you. Sometimes when Kirk and I are going down the road, people come around us for no reason and give us a hand signal, and it's not a wave – and you wonder what you've done wrong. I can remember a friend of ours who is prophetic traveled around the country during one of the presidential elections years ago. He took a trailer with a cross on the back of it and had Carman's song, "This Blood Is for You" blasting through the speakers.

He went all over America and drove around every capitol in every state seven times. When he was coming across New Mexico out in the desert area, no one was around, and suddenly a car came out of nowhere from behind him. As the car went around, the driver gave the finger sign to the cross as he went around. Our friend got angry, of which he never did, and stuck his head out his window and yelled, "Yes, it doesn't matter which finger you use, He's still number one!" What that first man was doing was probably demonically controlled.

I have too much fear of God to do something like that. Even when I was in witchcraft, I still had enough fear of God that I would not do something like that. You don't have to do anything to get them to rise up. Have you ever walked past someone in a store, and they act mad at you or growl or something? You know they are there, and you don't know what to do, since you are in the middle of a grocery store. Normally, you don't walk up in a grocery store and begin to cast out demons! You must have discernment.

I have seen demons screaming at little kids through their parents. I have seen them beat on them and cuss them out in public. You will know when it is an evil force that is not just flesh. Not everything is demonic, but you will know when it is demonic. They will let you know sometimes. In demonic possession, there is little or no control. Their will has been taken and they have little or no control over their body or actions. Their will has been captured by the enemy. This is when it is possession.

People don't know that they can have demonic things in their life hanging on. Not everyone is possessed, but you can still have demonic controls in your life on habits or situations or weaknesses that you still have. Christians are not possessed, but you can be demonized –that is a different thing than possession altogether. When someone is really possessed, they have no control over their own will. Devils are the worst for that. Demons usually come in sevens. I don't know why that is, but everywhere I have dealt with it, they usually come in groups of sevens. Whenever you are praying for people and think they are being delivered, they may have more than one. I always put my hand on someone's belly, because you can barely touch someone in their stomach area if they are possessed, and they will immediately begin to express pain or hurt. I normally put my hand there or have somebody that I know is qualified or living a righteous life. When you lay hands on them, the Spirit of God in you will touch their flesh, and they will feel it. A devil is different than a demon. It is fierce, cruel, and works to possess the mind. That's why people possessed with devils end up in mental institutions or mentally incapacitated in many cases.

I'm not saying that all mental issues means it is a devil, but sometimes you are fighting a devil. That is harder to get rid of than a demon. I don't have a clue why, but believe it is because it is in their mind and their will. You have to fight all of that, where a demon has to bow their knee at the Name of Jesus. A devil will wrap itself around the mind attempting to control the mind; therefore, you will find that you are dealing with the human elements and will need to get to the person as well as the devil. The person often feels trapped and hopeless and you must help them to believe that greater is He that is in you than he that is controlling them and their mind.

People who have devils will grab themselves in very specific personal areas or maybe expose themselves. A devil wants to expose its power some way through the person, and a lot of times they have no control over it. When a devil gets in the mind, it controls things like mental illness, depression, suppression. They end up isolated. You have to put them away somewhere. If nobody gets to them, they are that way the rest of their lives.

The demons are usually controlling things like lust. Lust is different than pornography when dealing with demonic control. Pornography is of the brain. Lust can cause that to be possessed, but I am saying lustful spirits usually deal demonically in the flesh. Anything that works with the brain is harder to cast out than that which deals just with the body.

We met a young girl years ago that was possessed by devils. That little sweet girl was beautiful when we met her. She was 12 when we first met her. There had been some guys that would come and take her out the window of her house. The mother had seen this happen and said she was too scared to do anything about it. The little girl told me things like 13 black men made me do horrible sexual things to them all night long. I eventually realized that it was not black men, it was men in black. There were 13 of them. They were taking her to a coven meeting. They took her repeatedly. By the time we got to her, her mind was so ingrained with devils that she was all but shut down in her thinking; however, she could draw. I took her drawings to a hospital where a lady knows how to discern drawings (she works with the police), and she confirmed what I believed about the coven as well. At one time, we took her to a home, and she was sitting in a room alone talking to something. She could not speak to me even when I commanded her to in the Name of Jesus. I prayed to God to ask Him why she couldn't speak. I believe it was a mute spirit that would overtake her to silence her. Could it be that in Heaven when the demons fell, God told some of them they would never speak or hear again? The Bible speaks of mute spirits. We did all we could do for her. The little girl was happy to be put in an institution. Demon possessed people are happy to be alone because they are so tormented when they try to get help.

The torment gets worse reaching out to Christians. If you lay hands on a demon possessed person and they don't get delivered, we must back away and begin to fast and pray. If you start praying for them but don't finish what you started, you will make it worse than it was before they came to you. The spirits will torment them worse.

Many times, there are unclean spirits that Christians don't even know are there. I went into a home once. The husband was so mean to his wife. She came to work while she was pregnant with her fourth baby. Her nose was swollen all over her face and she had two big black eyes. Her husband had come home from work the night before, was drunk and woke her up by smashing her face. I was broken for her. She asked me to pray over her house. We walked into the house and it was so messed up. It looked as if it hadn't been swept in months, there were little bits of trash everywhere, and the children's rooms were filthy. It stunk and there was animal excrement lying around. We went through the house and anointed the whole house, played praise and worship and cast everything out. We felt something happen. There was a change in the atmosphere of that house. We took it another step further. We went back the next day and cleaned her house. By the time we got back, she was already cleaning on it. We never saw her house that way again.

Did the husband get delivered? No, but he did leave her eventually. She went on to find a Godly man and marry him, and he cared for her children and her. Last time I heard, she was going to church and everything was fine. Unclean spirits can grab hold of houses and people. Sometimes it's spirits. Sometimes it's lazy people. Again, discernment.

Some people with demonic activity will have spastic actions. I have had people brought to me at the altar, and they get really spastic before they ever get to us. Often falling on the floor, and even have seen them move like a snake, or hiss. Foam starts coming out of their mouth. I have even seen them levitate off the floor while you are praying for them. That's in churches! We were in one church, and I prayed for a young man. He was foaming, and his eyes were like hot coals. He was totally delivered. He finally sunk back and began to sob, as he was totally freed. A girl was getting prayer, and she began to levitate. I called one of the associate pastors to help me pray. He told me to never do that again. He told us they don't do that in their church. They have never had us back. I just did what I knew to do to free them and had no idea that the pastor did not want it done, as it was a full gospel church. It makes you wonder if they know what "full gospel" and being filled with the Holy Spirit really means.

Oppression always comes before depression. You will find oppression will come to the point that you fall into depression. When you get to oppression, run to the altar, call your pastor or Christian friends to pray. If you don't take care of oppression, you will end up in depression. Is that demonic? Not inside, but outside, usually. I went to the movies with my grandkids one night. My grandson was feeling down, so we went to a movie. It was funny, and we laughed. It was such a delightful evening! If you think that there is any kind of depression or oppression with someone, get them somewhere they can laugh. Laughter doeth good like a medicine. When we got out of the movie, my grandson felt better. If I start feeling oppression coming or I'm going through something, I will turn on the TV and watch *Home Alone* and scream and laugh like crazy! That will get rid of where you are. Don't only Word them to pieces or pray for them. Let them laugh! Sometimes we can do natural things to back the enemy off. We are powerful. Sometimes we just need to be natural and know who we are in Jesus Christ and who He is in us.

Recognize what is a natural circumstance and what is a test of fire and your faith. Sometimes we are going through something that we don't know if it's God or the devil. Sometime it feels like the devil, but it could be God. It could be a test, and not deliverance. It could be a need for inner healing. When people are not reading the Word and praying, they can get oppressed. If you can get them back in the Word, they will usually snap out of it. They get their mind on the words of the natural instead of getting into the supernatural Word of God that is the only truth.

Depression can look like possession, but the demons are on the outside. They are tormenting spirits, talking in your ears. Sometimes if people have seen a bad movie or bad wreck, that torment stays with them and causes them to get oppressed. That is on the outside. Depression and oppression will make you do awful things that you would not normally do. You can counsel someone out of depression. The most wonderful thing to counsel them with before you get to the Word is a joyful face, a big hug and a lot of love. Love will heal them. Don't counsel people mad – "What does the Word say? Why do you feel that way? You know better than that!" No they don't, or they wouldn't be hurting! You go in and tell them, "I just want to tell you I love you". Sometimes people get delivered at the altar with me holding them and letting them cry.

A lady came to the altar 29 years ago. She went down to the floor. God spoke to me that she had never had a mother's arms around her like she needed. He told me to love the child within her. I held her in my lap and gave her a mother's heart's blessing. I loved her and told her "its ok, baby, just cry. Get it out". At one time she had even lived in a barn with her parents, one of whom was an alcoholic and the other was always out running with different men. She and her siblings were so neglected and abandoned so much that they all ended up in foster care. Her life was really rough, as she was sexually abused most of her life and rejected. She was absolutely set free by love. Love delivered her, and she has been growing by leaps and bounds for Christ! I could have stood there and bound up things and cast them out, and she wouldn't have been healed. She didn't need deliverance, she needed someone to love her and tell her she is worth something. Sometimes you can help somebody get out of that place where demons are trying to bind them up, just by loving them.

Truth will make you free. You have to get a person in position through prayer and sometimes counseling, that you can get the truth in them where it is real. They will reject truth because they don't know that truth will set them free. You know it, and sometimes you have to be brutal with it. You have to get them to the place that they can trust you to be brutal with them, and yet they know it is love. Truth hurts sometimes if it comes out wrong. And then you get mad, and then you want to get even. God says you have to forgive right away, because He knows the enemy will come in to a situation and make it worse if you don't stop that process.

I have dealt with many multiple personality disorders. Everyone wants to believe that multiple personality disorders are demonic (and in a sense, it is), but that is not always true. Sometimes people split. They get raped, molested, have incest in their family, saw a horrible wreck, been beaten by objects and words, etc. They split into different personalities to escape their reality. When that happens, it is a hard one. Find someone to help you who understands what they are doing. Every one of their personalities can be possessed. It gets sticky. I don't play that game. A lot of counselors and ministers will "play" with somebody for 20 years and never get them healed. I saw one on Oprah Winfrey that had 100 personalities. Oprah and she discussed, "Let's just not worry about it and get along with all of them". She said, "That's what I'm being trained to do." I have news for you – you were born one person, and God wants to bring you back to the host person that you are. You may not want to come back, because it hurts.

As a little girl, the person that mistreated me all the time would called me Prea. I didn't know whether it was better to be a boy or a girl. I found out that in Indonesia, Prea means "boy". I went back and studied that. The power of life and death is in the tongue, and that was a word curse. You can make your children and family subject to demonic powers because of the words you keep speaking over them.

I had a little girl come up to the altar one day and say, "I'm stupid". She was a beautiful little blonde-headed girl who was in foster care. I looked at her and said, "Baby, you are not stupid." I asked her who told her that. She told me her mom did, and said that she and her daddy didn't want her. She made F's in school all the time. She was in special education. We prayed and broke that curse. The next time we were in that church, that little girl was an A-B student and was out of special education.

Sometimes you have to realize that we have to heal memories in people. Some of them have had demonic oppression in them and maybe possession. Demons love our bad, unhealed memories. Demonic powers will come into damaged emotions and try to make a person a captive. When I pray for people, I will break every ancestral curse. **(Numbers 14:18)** Even though those curses have been forgiven, sometimes they have allowed demonic powers to come into those places. Alcoholism is not a curse from God! It has run down through the system of our families. I have broken that and cast out demons out of the bloodline, and there is no one else alcoholic afterward. I had incest in my family, and the Lord directed me to break that curse off my bloodline. One of my family members came to me at a family reunion right after that and told me he got saved.

It takes a period of time sometimes, and takes someone loving and caring to get the job done. Sometimes you have to talk to the people. I don't talk to demons, and I don't war with them verbally. When you take someone through deliverance that isn't totally possessed, sometimes, I will back off and find out the root of where that thing came in. The way to do that is to talk to the person and find out what happened to open that door or give the demon legal ground that causes the demon to think it doesn't have to leave. There was an open door somewhere, and you need to find that.

God has given us pastors, evangelists, apostles, teachers and prophets to teach us and to train us. They are supposed to be doing that, but I think today, they are just trying to grow churches. We are to equip the saints. If we finally get equipped, we come into unity. God knows we must have unity, because if we don't, we have no power to do anything. That is what is wrong with the church today. We have to come into spiritual unity, not only earthly unity.

There was a pastor and an evangelist who wanted me to stand by in case they needed me. They were casting the demons out of a little girl, and the demons were tearing her up. Her little stomach was almost like a baby was inside her, just fighting. They weren't getting it done. They asked me what to do. I told them, "This doesn't come about but by much fasting and prayer." I told them the church is going to have to fast and pray for this child. I ran into them a few weeks later and asked if they got the little girl delivered. They said, "No, and we fasted. " One of them said, "I gave up pop". The other one said, "I said I wouldn't eat cookies for 3 days". I just looked at them and walked away. When you are going into warfare, you don't eat. You fast for 3 days. You are not going to work with me unless you go on a fast for 3 days when I'm in a real situation of possession. I want you to pray and fast, and pray for you. I want you to clean you out. I won't work with people unless you are obedient.

Matthew 17:20. " So Jesus said to them, because of your unbelief, for surely I say to you, if you have faith as a grain of mustard seed, you will say to this mountain, move from here to there, and it will move and nothing will be impossible to you. However, this kind does not go out except by prayer and fasting."

The church must get to the place that they realize that nothing is impossible for us to do in Christ Jesus. We have faith and truth, but we still fight doubt and unbelief. If I walk in and someone is in a wheelchair, I hope they get out, but I don't know they are going to get out. I want to know that I know that I know that when I pray for them, it is done.

We have to be serious. One time when I was first going into ministry, I had a bunch of people in church with me. They were all of the "Spirit-filled" people in my non-Spirit-filled church that I went to for 9 years. They turned on me. They were jealous because I went on Lester Sumrall's television program and God was beginning to use me in ministry. I couldn't believe it was jealousy because it was my peers. I thought they were just holy people. They started calling me a witch, and saying I was no good, of the devil, still possessed, still had demons, wasn't totally delivered. I about lost my mind. The bishop and the young pastor of that denomination believed in me. They just wouldn't hear of it. Those people came back five years later, one in particular – my friend for many years, came back and apologized to me and told me "I was so wrong." She still called me "Nellie". People won't let you get past where they want you. Some people can't receive who I am today. They can only receive me when they left me back there. I will always remain that person to them, because whatever their problem, they won't let me be what I am today. You must just love them, because they won't go any further until they allow others to go further. I was always blaming myself for things going wrong. I didn't need the help of the devil. I would do it for him. Now, I really don't care who thinks what of me. I have been wounded a lot because I'm a woman, but I know that I know that if I have Jesus, I will not allow anyone to steal that from me anymore. I have missed major opportunities because of fear and doubt – not of God, but of Janelle. That is where the church is now. We are still too much into our own selves, and not enough into God. Some of those folks from that church are not even in church anymore, and some have faced terrible trials. My heart goes out to them.

Everything we do is not just in the Name of Jesus; it is in the NATURE of Jesus and who He is. **Luke 10:20** "Do not rejoice in this, that the spirits are subject to you, but rather rejoice because your names are written in Heaven." Too many people in deliverance ministry love it when demons and people fall at their feet and foam at the mouth, and they have the power over them. Don't! I am not glad I was in witchcraft, but I will tell you that because of those things I was and did, when I met Jesus, I knew it was all about Him. It had very little to do with Janelle. In ministry, He gets all the glory, because I know what I am capable of. I wanted to be the nature of Jesus and wanted to be like Him. I still do, and I still work toward that. I don't work toward that so I can have the power, but so I can show the power of who He is.

Five people are what I told you to get when you go into deliverance ministry. Of those five, I want one praise warrior. I want somebody, if there's a real demon-possessed person, to just get in the corner and just be praising Jesus. They don't have to pray, give me discernment, get a word from God – they just need to use their gift of praising Jesus, getting in His Presence and to usher in the power. Demons hate it! They hate praise! I want one person that is a prayer warrior, praying at all times. I want them in the room praying, praying in tongues if they have that gift. Pray, pray, pray! Sometimes when nothing seems to be happening, I put my hand on the person and begin to praise Jesus. I lose myself in the praises of Jesus. The demons begin to shrink back. They know I am in the Throne Room and God has inhabited me and His praises, and they can't stay. Praises literally cast demons out! I need someone well-versed in the Word. I know the Word and read it constantly but I am not good at quoting the Word. I won't give drugs or anything credit. I know it, but to quote it verbatim, I am not good at it. I always want someone well-versed in the Word, or someone who can look it up quickly. Demonic powers will try to mess you up on that, because they know it and will try to make you look stupid with it. You must have someone who knows the Word. Jesus defeated the devil with one thing—the Word. It was always, "IT IS WRITTEN". If you don't have it written on your heart and mind, don't mess with anyone who is possessed. That is the biggest thing in the world that you need to know is the Word. You have to know where you are in the Word and where you place these people in the Word, and you have to know what God is saying for you to do and what He is telling these demons to do. You cannot go into deliverance ministry if you do not have the Word in you! Stay out of the room and back off, for your own protection.

You cannot have fear. Perfect love casts out all fear. You cannot take fear in the room with you. Demons love fear and worry. Don't give me a worry-wart to take in that room with me. That is lack of faith and unbelief. I fight with that myself; I don't need yours to fight with. I get mine under the Blood before I get in there! I'm so human. I know what it's like living this life for Jesus. We all have worries and frets and problems that we have to go through and get rid of when we are going into battle. You have to have perfect love for the person you are dealing with. How? You don't go in with your momma you hate and have lots of issues with and think you are going to cast out a demon. You have to get yourself in perfect love. Leave that to someone else. Those demons will tear you up. **Luke 10:19** says "All authority has been given to you." ALL authority, not just a little bit. I have all the authority of Heaven, and that irritates some Christians. They think you are being high-minded when you say, "I count myself equal with Jesus Christ." He said "I am a joint heir with Him." He is not jealous of us. He wants us to do greater things than He did, because He went to the Father. What is wrong with us? We are so jealous of each other that we think Jesus is jealous of us!

A house divided cannot stand. If we are in a room with someone that is possessed, and we begin to get jealous of one another or I think, "I know it more than the leader", then the house will be divided, and the enemy will try to come in like a flood and take it. You don't have all the gifts. You don't have all the fruit harvested yet. We need each other. We need the giftings and calls in each person. But there is a training time that some people are not ready for yet. If I see someone coming up and laying hands on someone in the church, if I know that there are demonic powers at work, I will take their hands and ask them to stand to the side and pray. Some people have gotten their feelings hurt and walked away – they just have to. I go to them later and explain to them that they didn't do anything wrong. I just don't want any transference of spirits, and I don't want any problems, and I need unity, and I don't know you. Every pastor should have altar people. They need to make sure they are in agreement, that they don't have issues against them. Not everybody should be up there ministering to people.

Remember, one will chase 1,000 to flight. Two will chase 10,000 to flight. We need each other! It is all about Jesus, and not about us.

Matthew 18:10 "Again, I say to you that if two of you agree on earth concerning anything that they ask, it will be done for them by my Father in Heaven."

Verse 20, "For where two or three are gathered together in my Name (His nature of

LOVE), I am there in the midst of them."

Repent of any sin and check your armor. If you have holes in your armor or you have laid a piece of it down, you may get attacked. The enemy can see what you can't see. I went up to a demon we were casting out one day. This voice came out of this woman, and it was a man's voice. It said, "Where are your children?" I had one in Hawaii in service that was telling me he was sitting out on mines trying to let one blow up on him because his girlfriend had broken up with him, and he didn't want to live anymore for a little bit. I had two others at home that were not serving God. When it looked at me, it said, "I know where they are and I have got them!" You better know God and know the promises of God. I began to say, "God has them. My sons are fine!" I could not let worry and fear in. If you have covered your children with prayer, they are covered. I had a grandson to die of SIDS/crib death. You see, was that demonic? I don't know what it is, but I learned how to trust God really quickly! This is just temporal and short-term. I still have a grandson. He is in Heaven waiting on Grandma. I can't concern myself with that because then I'd get mad at God, and I would have enmity with Him. Then I would be of no good to anybody here on earth. It gives power to the enemy when you worry.

God says, "My church is having all the trouble because my people are always trying to take authority over one another that they don't have. The only authority I give you is over the enemy." We are not supposed to be enemies. Denominations have helped in making us enemies. Just people and personalities do that too. How do we do it? I can't tell you, but you better get in unity. You better love one another, because we do not have authority over one another. If you have an enemy barking at your back door, or messing with your emotions or doubt and unbelief, I can take authority. But I have no authority over you, and I'm not better than any of you. You are a brother and sister, and that's where it's at.

Guard your thought life. **II Corinthians 10:4-5** "For the weapons of our warfare are not carnal, but mighty in God for pulling down strongholds, casting down arguments and every high thing that exalts itself against the knowledge of God, bringing every thought into captivity to the obedience of Christ."

That is why people that have watched something like porn, murder or rape, then they act out certain things. They did not guard their mind. I do not watch movies where girls get raped, or movies that have children being sexually, physically or verbally abused. Why? I live it over and over again for days and weeks, and I'm angry and upset at the people who did it. I won't put myself through that. I don't watch things on witchcraft and the occult. Why? I don't let those things in here to me. If I do, they can set up a little throne in there, and I don't need that. In the Bible, **Romans 8**, it says "The carnal mind is enmity against God, because it is not subject to the law of God nor indeed can be. So then, those who are in the flesh cannot please God." Carnal man cannot cast out spiritual demons. If you are in carnality, you are already in enmity with God, and you can get in trouble.

Matthew 24:35 says "Heaven and Earth will pass away, but my Word will by no means pass away." Get that in your heart. It is the Word of God.

Isaiah 55:11 (one of my favorite Scriptures) "So shall my Word be that goes forth from My mouth. It shall not return to Me void, but it shall accomplish what I please and it shall prosper in the thing of which I sent it." Mark that. Eat that Word!

A young lady had a homosexual spirit and they couldn't get her delivered. She started foaming at the mouth when I went to her. I said, "I bind that homosexual spirit up in the Name of Jesus". They couldn't get her delivered, and that was the thing that was stopping her. I bound it up, and it started growling and twisting and wanting me to die. I had to stand on the Word. Fear wanted to grab me. I couldn't move for a minute. A man bound the demons up, and I went on. The demonic hold on her was trying to come after me. Once in a while, if you have had incest or bad things happen to you, sometimes that spirit of evil that is there will try to back you off because of what has happened to you. What you need to do is back off and get prayer or go pray or praise and get your strength back. Demons are created beings. They can't destroy God. They would love to, but they can't. He is God and their Creator. If they could destroy Him, they would in turn destroy themselves.

God has no beginning. Heaven is there forever. Have you ever tried to figure out how far the sky goes? My oldest son was so smart. We would have these little talks at bedtime. He would always ask me, "Mom, how long is eternity? When does it end?

What is after Heaven?" I don't know how big God is, but He is the I AM. There is no beginning and no end to God. There is going to be an end to Satan, and it makes him mad. He thought there would be an end to Jesus at Calvary and that he would destroy Jesus, but he didn't. He just had his own fate sealed.

Should all believers cast out demons? **Mark 16:17** "These signs will follow those that believe. In my Name, they will cast out demons; they will speak in new tongues."

John 14:12, 14 "Most assuredly, I say to you, he who believes in Me, the works that I do, he will do also and greater works than these will he do because I go to my Father. Whatever you ask in My Name, that I will do that the Father may be glorified in the Son. If you ask anything in My Name, I will do it."

That "I" is GOD. God will do it. We just come in His Name, but God will do it. It is not our fault if people don't get this or that. We blame ourselves. Just keep praying!

Jesus cast out demons. He never did a miracle until He was filled with the Holy Spirit. Then He started doing miracles. That same Holy Spirit that lived in Him now lives in us! Why aren't we just walking around doing it? The same Spirit in Jesus that cast demons out now lives in us. We have the authority and we have the power. Let's just get busy.

Some people say that was only for the beginning of the church, to prove it was real. I look at them and say, "Then I don't need to be saved today because it was the beginning of the church". It is not true! It was the beginning of the church, but not the end!

Stay balanced. God told me that the church has been hearing a lot of men's thoughts of the Word, and not reading the Word, and we have become unbalanced by our inner ear. We have too much in it that is not the Word of God; it is the word of man talking about the Word of God – parables. We have to watch out for that. Get more teaching, always learning.

The Bible says a lot of people are ever learning, but never coming to the Truth. You must ask God for the truth. Lift up the Name of Jesus. That is where the Holy Spirit will run to – the Name of Jesus. The Holy Spirit only moves on the Word of God, only moves on Jesus. We wonder why we aren't seeing more revival—I think we have preached every story and used every interpretation and we need to get back to the message of Jesus Christ. Billy Graham has never had a service that he didn't see thousands come to Jesus.

Who did he lift up? Jesus! Holy Spirit runs to the Name of Jesus.

I Corinthians 14:1 "Pursue love and desire spiritual gifts." Pursue love. That means find love. Desire all the rest, but we have to get back to where we pursue love. Thank God for the gifts, but we must pursue love.

Matthew 10:7-8. "As you go, preach, saying the kingdom of Heaven is at hand. Heal the sick, cleanse the lepers, raise the dead, cast out demons. Freely you have received, freely give." He commissions us to do it.

Don't shut up your watch dogs! Don't muzzle them! There should be a good watch dog in every flock. There was never a good shepherd anywhere that didn't first go get them a dog. But if the dog starts eating the sheep, kick them out. There are people that are watchdogs that begin to eat and hurt the sheep. They do have extra senses and smell the enemy before they see him. They do hear him coming before anybody knows he is there, but they must be careful that they know who the enemy is and they aren't sheep eaters. If they are, the shepherd has to destroy them. What is a watchdog? Most of the time, it's the pastor's wife! "Honey, I don't trust that person. You better watch that one, Honey!"

We need someone to say, "It's the enemy! It's a wolf in sheep's clothing." Instead, they get mad at the dog and kick it. The dog will stick around. The person in your church that's been more faithful than anybody, they will stick around and stick by you. You are their shepherd and they love you. Let them come out of the corner. Go have coffee with them and tell them to talk to you. Listen to them. Churches today have silenced the prophetic utterance of God and the watchdog. They are getting in trouble and getting their sheep killed because nobody lets it come forth. Use the five-fold ministry for the equipping of the saints. There are people in your church that know and can help. Don't silence them. Train them!

Be perfect and holy. The Bible says, "Be holy just as I am holy." He wants us to be holy. Holy is like Him.

You have to know that nothing can separate us from the knowledge of God. Nothing! **Hebrews 13:5** says "He will never forsake you nor leave you." Stand on His Word. **Matthew 28:18** says "All authority has been given to you." He gave it to you. Jesus is not jealous of us. Always remember that!

You have to know that God loves you and He wants you to move and work in all of this.

He does not want you to be distressed or afraid. He will give you a word. I have given words to people and said, "Do this and do that. Don't do this, do that." People have given me words. That is how this book came into being. Three different prophets in different parts of the country told us, "I see you stationary a little bit, and you are supposed to do something." I ignored them. I had a prophetess/pastor call. She said, "I have a directive message for you. She started talking and said, "Start this in your home. Find a way. God wants you to do something in your home." I was saying in my mind, "I can't, God. She couldn't see me, but said, "Janelle! You CAN! Start it! God will bring them!" So this is how this teaching and instructions came about, I listened and obeyed, with confirmation from God.

Sometimes people that are prophetic will tell you things that you don't want to hear. If you are hateful, angry, mean and grouchy, they will tell you that too. They love you enough to tell you that you need to change. It is not to hurt you, but to make you the nature of Jesus Christ so that you will have all power and not be afraid!

They are getting you to the greater works that God has planned for you.

When God spoke to me about having a meeting in our home on Tuesday nights a few years ago, I didn't know what to minister and teach on. Holy Spirit spoke to me and told me to teach on demons and deliverance. I cried out to Him and said, "I lost that teaching years ago." Of course, just a few days later I ran into those teachings that were so old they were still on cassette tapes. I groaned and accepted the assignment, knowing that most don't want to know the things that are in this teaching and now this book.

We continued to travel and we were astonished how our itinerary made it possible to be home on Tuesday nights for almost 10 months. The few nights that we were unable to be home, there were good ministers and teachers that filled in. Many people and ministers from other states came at one time or another, the most we had in our front room at one time was forty-five. We were packed out. God moved after every teaching wonderfully. People still talk about this teaching and how it helped them to grow and understand how to minister to people who are oppressed by demonic activity. **Luke 4:18** came alive in the people as a personal assignment from God. "The Spirit of the Lord is upon Me, Because He has anointed

Me to preach the gospel to the poor; He has sent Me to heal the brokenhearted, to proclaim liberty to the captives and recovery of sight to the blind, to set at liberty those who are oppressed;" In **John 14:12** Jesus said; "Most assuredly, I say to you, he who believes in Me, the works that I do he will do also; and greater works than these he will do, because I go to My Father." Jesus wants us to do what He did.

Authority of the Believer. I was thinking one day (I'm not saying this was God) about Lucifer in Heaven when he was an angel. The angels had to have had a will. Lucifer had to have a will in Heaven. I think after Lucifer and the angels fell, could it be that the rest of them just looked at God and asked Him to take their will away? I don't know what happened, but I do know that we all have a will. We have a will, we have our own righteousness, and we have our own self-centeredness. We have to watch that as Christians. We are not going to quit dwelling in this flesh until it dies. The stronger you get in the Word and it in you, the less authority and strength your flesh has over you. When you are a new Christian, many times it is not demonic. It is your flesh that you have to discern between which is flesh and which is a demonic power. No matter what you are going through, you have the authority. "The devil made me do it" is a lie!

In **Luke 10:18,** Jesus said, "I saw Satan fall like lightning from Heaven." Jesus was very aware that Satan fell out of Heaven. I want you to see where he came from. In Heaven, he guarded the treasures of Heaven. He was beautiful. Most theologians believe the King of Tyre is a description of Satan. You have to make sure that what you have is a gift from God that belongs to Him – not you. Satan fell from Heaven and came to earth. Until we realize there is an enemy on this earth, we will have no reason for authority. Many Christians do not walk in authority over their flesh and over the powers that be on this earth because they really don't believe that there is an enemy outside their body in the spirit realm. They lack things they need spiritually because they don't believe they have an enemy.

We have a will. When we came to Jesus, we gave it back to Him. We are the fruit of Jesus Christ. Jesus bore you in travail. You are His fruit. Why are we the fruit? We are hanging on the Vine.

Luke 10:19-20. "Behold I give you the authority to trample on serpents and scorpions and over all the power of the enemy, and **nothing** shall by any means hurt you." Then why do we get hurt? This is referring to spiritual wounds. We can get to the place in Jesus Christ that our mind is stayed on heavenly places and whatever we gain or lose doesn't matter. We are still whole in Jesus Christ.

"Nevertheless, do not rejoice in this, that

the spirits are subject to you, but rather rejoice that your names are written in Heaven." I have seen people throw up spiders and things that look like animals. I have seen people contort and look awful. I've seen them slobber, gag, puke, call me filthy names, take out gobs of slime out of their mouth. I've seen it all – maybe not all, but I've seen enough! I had a former high priest from Satanism tell me, "I'm so glad you are out of witchcraft. I would be terrified of you. You are one powerful lady!" The power was not me. Why? Because I know Jesus and I know if He can set me free and heal me, then He can do it for anybody! I looked him in the eyes and said, "You don't need to be afraid of me, but Who is in me. At His Name the enemy has to flee or bow the knee." His eyes turned to terror at the Name of Jesus. If I never cast out a demon and neither do you, your name is written in the Lamb's Book of Life and you have a right to this authority that God is talking about.

The spirits are subject to you and I. Don't make them big, huge – NO. They are subject to you and I. They have to do what we tell them to do as long as we come in the Name and character of Jesus. Having this authority and power, we should be grateful and humbled to have it, because this power we have in us to do signs and wonders and cast out demons is to bring forth the glory of God! The authority that you have in you – Jesus suffered and died in agony and travailed so you could have that authority. How dare you or I take any of the glory for that! We have suffered nothing like Jesus Christ suffered so we could have His authority, His love, His salvation. We ALL have it! We have begun to look for the person who has it instead of looking unto Jesus, who gave it to ALL of us. Why is it that people in ministry always think their ministry is the greatest? There is no place for competition and jealousy in the Body of Christ! We have to stop the nonsense of comparing ministry to ministry. We cannot glory in man anymore!

Again, I have been on *TBN*, *700 Club*, *Lester Sumrall*, *Geraldo Rivera Show*, spoken in many major colleges across the country, been in *USA Today*, and many other magazines and papers, but NONE of these do one thing for your ministry! When you try to build your own ministry, it will not work. It must be Jesus and His authority, His power and His love. We need to slide down on our knees and ask the Holy Spirit to promote us for the glory and cause of Christ.

Luke 10:19 – the devil has power. Don't fool yourself that he doesn't have any power. I will not glorify him, but he does have power, or we wouldn't need any. What he doesn't have is AUTHORITY. We have been given all power and authority over him! When you are in sin, in doubt, trust issues with God, fear, worry, low self-esteem, self-guilt, self-pity, these are the weapons that Satan uses against us. He uses what is already within us as weapons. This is why we need inner healing and even deliverance from self. Can Christians be possessed? I have seen Christians possessed with jealousy, unforgiveness, and bitterness. You can cast it out 24 hours a day, 7 days a week for 20 years and it will never change until you REPENT. Through repentance, you can be healed of these things!

Some people have more power in different areas than you do. They have learned authority because of their knowledge of the Word and the experiences they have had that made them need that knowledge. They have the truth and the Spirit. You can have the Spirit and not the truth. You can be baptized in the Holy Spirit and reject the truth (it is painful sometimes, so people reject it), so the Spirit of God starts to become dormant. If you don't believe it, read the Word that says, **Ephesians 4:30** "Grieve not the Holy Spirit" and **1 Thessalonians 5:19** states "Do not quench the Spirit." You have Christians not living up to their potential because they have hate in their heart, stopping the move of the Holy Spirit. Wash your mind with the truth – use the Word of God. People have had to take the authority or have stayed in teaching, seeking wisdom. Authority has wisdom with it. If you don't have wisdom to go with authority, why have it? You will destroy your own ministries, walk, and reputation without wisdom. If you have the word of knowledge and you don't have the word of wisdom to go with it, watch out. You can know lots of things through the word of knowledge, but you need wisdom to know what to do with it. Sometimes, it is just to pray, but not to speak it out. You may never know they get delivered, but they may – and it won't be you! Some of authority is learned, and wisdom is too. Don't think you don't need preaching and teaching or that you don't need someone else's. You need wisdom from people who may be stronger than you and more knowledgeable in the Word.

Seasoned Christians know their authority and they become unshakeable in the Word of

God and the word of faith. They know authority and wisdom and have been seasoned in it. There is nothing like wonderful beef stew or chili, but it's better the longer you cook it on the back burner – that's how it is with a seasoned Christian.

I Corinthians 12:4-5, "There are diversities of gifts but the same Spirit; there are differences of ministries, but the same Lord." Stop thinking you are the only one! We need each other. Your gift may seem insignificant to you, but I may need it badly to come near to me. If you have a ministry, don't think that you are the best. God has many different ministers. If I died tomorrow, someone would take my place. He is the only One!

Pastors used to say, "She has a deliverance ministry" and pastors wouldn't let me come because they didn't want the deliverance ministry. I don't have a deliverance ministry, I just walk in it! When Jesus told us to go, He told us to walk in it! There is no such thing as a healing "ministry". Jesus told us it's our commission! If we stop lifting up a person (instead of Jesus) that has those kinds of gifts, we might see signs and wonders flow in the Body of Christ. There is a healing gift, but I'm talking about ministry – He has given us all the authority to go forth and do everything that He did. He wills us to do these things. There is no gift or any place you can find to cast out demons and get smarter on doing it. You just speak His words and He is the One with the power. **1John 4:4** "You are of God, little children, and have overcome them, because He who is in you is greater than he who is in the world." The nature of Jesus in you brings forth that power in you. Don't let the gift in you overpower someone else that doesn't have your gifting. Don't say such things as "If you had faith like me, you wouldn't get sick. You wouldn't need money," etc. This is caused by pride, and we know that earlier we read in Proverbs that pride goes before destruction. Esteem all your brothers and sisters better than yourself.

When I go into churches, I feel out the pastor, if I have time. I try to listen to the church and the people, and I find the heartbeat of where I am. That is why I go into the churches to minister. I don't lead them into where I am. I find the heartbeat of where they are and stretch their faith. That is what Jesus did. If you don't do that, you will cause them to have a "heart attack" and you won't be able to go back; they will be afraid of you.

When you deal with the flesh, you have to have fasting and prayer days and get the mind of Jesus in you. You want to look and act just like Him. We should be making flesh mad at us for the truth instead of babysitting demonic powers in the flesh. Love is power, but we cannot love flesh over the Spirit. I can love you, but if I see you doing something wrong, I will correct you. Do I not correct my children and grandchildren? I want them to know the truth, and that truth will make them free.

I will not give you a word if God hasn't given it to me. If someone is hurting, hurt them with the love of truth—authority versus control. A lot of people think they are exercising authority when all they are doing is taking control. Ministers must be careful, as you are in a place of authority, but you must not take that as control. There are churches full of people who are being controlled. When people are looking to control or be controlled, they are looking for a Saul. It means they don't want to have to pay for their sins, as if someone else made them do it. You must have a personal relationship with Jesus so you have a choice whether to sin or not. Again I say, the devil didn't make you do anything. He has no authority over you as a child of God. He has power, but you may have given him your authority, and you need to get your authority back! Taking authority over others is fun, but taking authority over you is another story!

No head knowledge in counseling will cast out demons. You must get into the spirit where they are. You must be in a spiritual atmosphere to see it done. Warfare is not in the natural realm. It is the power of the Lord Jesus Christ. Some will try to do it in the natural, but we must be spiritually filled, spiritually walking and talking. Counseling is good, but counseling should just stir them up to realize they need deliverance from demonic powers. Counseling deals with the natural, but it takes the Spirit to cast out demons. It doesn't need to take 20 years of counseling to deal with demonic powers.

Emotions take healing. You cannot cast those out. You have to be healed emotionally, because those have been damaged. There is an inner healing; if not, why did Jesus say we would heal the broken hearts? Your heart is where the emotions lie, where the will is, where all the circumstances are that makes you who you are. God knew some of us needed to be healed. When I got saved and delivered of demons, I was all twisted inside.

When He set me free, I was healed inside, but He healed one thing, then another, then another, and ongoing until now. I really think that I am just about totally healed. I won't say 100%, but I feel like I am; however, I stay out of my past. He is such a gentleman, if He had healed me all at once, I probably would have gotten locked away somewhere insane, as I could not have faced all those areas at once. God is a perfect gentleman. He would never do anything to hurt us. Sometimes instant healing could hurt us, but God would never do that.

This is a five-finger exercise to use for ministering healing: Hold your hand up and look at your fingers, beginning with the thumb. The thumb is the only digit that can touch all the others. 1) The thumb represents Hurt; 2) the index finger represents anger; 3) the middle finger represents the need to get even, but you are not allowed to as a Christian; 4) the ring finger represents unforgiveness starts guarding you, and you hold people hostage; 5) the little finger represents bitterness. When bitterness comes in, that starts to cripple you. It spreads, and your hand becomes a fist. We have too many people in churches today that have a fist. You can't shake a hand extended to you when you have a fist balled up. To get people healed, you have to back up and touch the hurt. That is why many do not get healed in counseling-- because you get them to the point of the hurt/pain and they often stop because they don't want the pain. They walk away with it still packed up deep inside, with a fist that hurts others around them. Pain lets us know that something needs fixed. Remember, the thumb represents hurt and it touched all the other fingers. You must expect to hurt to heal.

Pray for discernment. Demons are sneaky and smart. I have met people who are nonbelievers who know the Word better than we do. The first thing they say is, "Don't be judgmental!" It isn't them that know the Word so well, but the devil knows the Word and twists it to use it against you. Just because someone speaks or preaches the Word, doesn't make them of God. You must be careful because some denominations and even churches can be almost occult in nature. Demons will mock you with the Word, and then laugh at you. Demons go to church! They like the church – that is where a war zone is. They have assignments against us. **1Peter 5:8** "Be sober, be vigilant; because your adversary the devil walks about like a roaring lion, seeking whom he may devour." Ancestral curses have demons with them. My cousin who did our ancestry told me that our great-great-uncle by marriage was one of our presidents. I found a little book years ago on the Masons. This uncle was a Mason. My great-great-aunt held séances in the White House. These were my relatives. This was in the blood line. They went to church!

The anti-Christ will fool even the very elect, according to the Word. There are a lot of people in churches today that are anti-Christ. The anti-Christ is against the anointing. A church that does not want the anointing will dry up and fall off the vine. You must have the Spirit of God!

Bind up the enemy-the strong man–the demon. I have seen the time that people have cast a spirit of rape out of someone, and that person goes out and rapes someone as it leaves, and they spend 20 years in prison. Don't just cast it out, but first bind them up. I have seen it happen. **Mark 16:17** tells us to cast out demons.

There are religious cultures and social orders where voodoo, witchcraft, and other occult practices are rampant, but no one in the church is casting these things out when they get saved. Everywhere we go, we are to cast out demons.

God is a jealous God. He does not tolerate any god before Him – especially ourselves!

I was in the den of my house one night, where I slept, The man I was married to at the time had left me right after I was born again. I could not stand to sleep in my room alone. Suddenly, this huge thing walked right out of the air. It was brown, with tattered clothing. It was growling and hissing, and told me, "You are mine. You have been promised!" I was paralyzed in fear and was unable to move. Deep inside of me, I screamed, "Jesus!" but nothing could come out of my mouth. I started to calm inside. About that time, one of the doors to the room opened, and in came a beautiful bright light with a sword. This was before *Star Wars*, by the way! It was floating, and it was over the top of this being. The demon kept screaming, "She's mine! She's been promised!" The spirit being said, "No. We gave her back her will and she chose God. You can never, ever, ever, ever have her again!" The whole scene disappeared, and I will be honest. As a young Christian alone with three boys asleep upstairs, I slept with the light on after that for many nights.

I asked my mother about where I had been promised. I looked for that promise. Some of you have been promised to a spirit, but when you get saved, that spirit has to go. There is no time in space, in the spirit realm. They never die, and they are after that blood line. I really think that could be some of what PMS is about. I have seen women healed of that because the demonic powers have been bound and cast away from them. Spirits don't age. Angels are attached to us, and demons do the same thing. They have assignments against us. Let us say that someone in our ancestral background was in witchcraft and was supposed to promise their child to the devil for some sort of bargaining power and could not give it. They said, "I will give you the child of my lineage of my great-great-great grandchild. Well that could be you. In the spirit realm there are no days, nights, weeks, months, or years, so they have no problem waiting.

My sweet, Godly mother told me this one day as I asked her if there was any witchcraft in our family that she knew of. She immediately firmly said, "No!" However, she said that her father (my grandfather) used to read the tarot cards for the mayor of their city and other city officials every year. She then said that was nothing. When he couldn't do it, her mother would read them for them. Then she further informed me that she too read them for people, and there was nothing wrong with it at the time. She was so innocent and defensive telling me about it. I just stopped talking about it to her, as she had no idea and was as holy as any saint can be.

Note: demons have a stench to them sometimes. Don't get sick doing deliverance. They will do anything to make you sick at your stomach when you are going thru the real deal. It can get messy.

We diffuse a fragrance in Christ. They smell Jesus in us when we walk around. We diffuse the fragrance of Jesus, and spirits do the opposite.

Authority means power to influence or command. Authority influences. You are influential. You have God's authority to be influential in people's lives. Control is to rule over, restrain or direct influence over people, to have power over people or circumstances. Authority cannot be broken because it is a covenant. You have it! We have the covenant for authority. The devil does NOT have it!

An example is a salt covenant, when two people mix salt together to signify their unbreakable bond and covenant. This is the kind of covenant Jesus makes with us – you can't pick out what is Him and what is you.

Are you an accredited Christian? Do you tithe? Do you love? Do you have kindness, forgiveness, working on harvesting all the fruit of the Spirit? When you take your wallet out to buy something (in the natural), the cashier wants your license. What's in your Christian wallet inside? What do people find when you introduce yourself? The enemy will try to steal your identity as a Christian. Don't let him. There are people who will steal who you are. They will drag on you and never get healed or set free and never do anything about their situation but talk to you – they will end up having your identity. They will try to steal your time. When God tells me who to pray for, I don't go to someone else. We have to be led of the Spirit. Don't let anyone push you to a different person to pray for until it's time.

Matthew 28:18 says, "All authority has been given to you in Heaven and on Earth." We have all authority because Jesus lives in us.

Luke 4:5-6 says "Then the devil took him up on a high mountain and showed him all the kingdoms of the world in a moment of time and the devil said to him, "All authority I will give you and their glory, for this has been delivered to me, and I give it to whomever I wish." He has some authority to give to people, and it is of the world – of the earth.

You have to be careful when you walk in authority, that it is God's authority and not an earthly, sensual authority. How do we get it? We get it by harvesting the fruit of the Spirit. The Bible says "pursue love and desire spiritual gifts." Love is Jesus. The gifts are the Holy Spirit. They are for us to do something with, but not to own anyone, control anyone, beat people up with them. They are to give us the power as well as the authority. He's such a good God!

Romans 8:31, "What then shall we say to these things? If God is for us, who can be against us? Who shall separate us from the love of Christ? Shall tribulation or distress or persecution or famine or nakedness or perils or sword? Yet in all these things, we are more than conquerors through Him who loved us."

I Corinthians 15:57, "But thanks be to God who gives us the victory through our Lord Jesus Christ. Greater is He that is in me than he who is in the world."

Philippians 2:10, "Every knee shall bow and every tongue confess that He is Lord."

We are more than conquerors because we have authority, and authority comes from the throne room where God dwells. He dwells in us, because we are His temple. You don't have to get something you already have!

II Timothy 1:7 "For God has not given us a spirit of fear, but of power and of love and of a sound mind." This scripture is one of my favorite scriptures that I hold on to.

SUMMARY OF SPIRITUAL WARFARE AND INSTRUCTIONS

In summarization, in spiritual warfare, you must first determine and discern which warfare you are in. Many people do not realize that there are two warzones in the Bible and that we seem to want everything to be the devil or an attack by demons. However, we are yet in the flesh and must stop demonizing our flesh and begin to acknowledge its temptations to fall into sin. Then we can deliver it from the wiles of the devil. The devil did not make you do it. The hidden sin of the heart, (core of who you are) caused you to do it.

In **2 Corinthians 10:3-6**, it speaks to us about a very present and real warzone that dwells within us in our soul realm. "For though we walk in the flesh do not war according to the flesh, for our weapons are not carnal but mighty in God for pulling down strongholds, casting down arguments and every high thing that exalts itself against the knowledge of God, bringing every thought into captivity to the obedience of Christ." Therefore, we must make our flesh submit to our spirit where the Spirit of God dwells in us.

In **James 2:19**, it states that "even the demons believe and tremble." You just can't believe in Christ Jesus and His saving grace. You have to establish His character in all that you do and are. Can we be perfect? No, but we should have a desire to strive to be.

Let me share a part of a message God taught me. I asked Him one day what gets saved when we repent and come to Him. Is it our body, soul, or spirit, or all three? You know, if you ask Holy Spirit a question and wait, He will answer you. Here is what He showed me. Our bodies are not redeemed until we die, and the moment we are conceived in our mother's womb, we are appointed to die. He showed me that when we repent and ask Jesus into our hearts, His Spirit unites with our spirit and begins the process of restoring our soul. Yes, our spirit and soul are born again and saved; however, our soul person has not gotten the mind and will of Christ yet, and that is where we get into troubles of the flesh.

The soul of man is the will, intellect, and emotions. This is where sanctification and circumcision of the flesh comes in. Our will has been to do what we will to do, and now we need the help of the Holy Spirit and the Word of God to train our will to be His will.

In doing so, we must feed our intellect the Word to wash our minds clean of what we have put in it during our lifetime of sin, and also what others have put in it during our natural growth process from birth. For our lives may have damaged emotions that circumstances such as word curses, abandonment, fears of all kinds, failures, damaged egos for men, abuses for both men and women, absence of love and the right correction, never being allowed to have an opinion, always controlled by others, and the list goes on.

Hear me. No, hear the Word of God! It is a must that you allow the healing touch of **Galatians 5:22-23** "But the fruit of the Spirit is love, joy, peace, longsuffering, kindness, goodness, faithfulness, gentleness, self control, Against such there is no law." I always teach that the fruit of the fruit of the Spirit is the last, "self control," as when you work on all the others you will find yourself more controlled by the Spirit of God than what your emotions tell you to do and feel. It will begin your journey to inner healing.

Inner healing will take you to the lowest valleys of who you are, and that is where we don't want to go. However, it is a must for those who want to be healed and restored.

Your soul is the part of you that only you and God can see into the deepest pits that are in you. It's your secret place, and if you allow God to enter, it will become a place of peace where you can run for refuge.

Isaiah 61:1-3 "The Spirit of the Lord God is upon me, Because the Lord has anointed Me to preach good tidings to the poor; He has sent Me to heal the broken hearted, to proclaim liberty to the captives, And the opening of the prison to those who are found; To proclaim the acceptable year of the Lord, And the day of vengeance of our God; To comfort all who mourn, To console those who mourn in Zion, To give them beauty for ashes, the oil of joy for mourning, The garment of praise for the spirit of heaviness; That they may be called trees of righteousness, The planting of the Lord, that He may be glorified." These scriptures came to life in Jesus, according to what Jesus spoke **in Luke 4:18-19**. This is the anointing that we now carry for others, but first for our inner selves. According to **Isaiah 61:4** "And they shall (which is us), rebuild the old ruins, They shall raise up the former desolations, And they shall repair the ruined cities, The desolations of many generations."

In other words, we are to be healed and delivered from every wound and power of scars that we have in us. This is so that we may become healers to others by the anointing that we carry and the mandate from God to go forth, especially to our families who may suffer from the same things we have suffered through.

Numbers 14:18 "The Lord is longsuffering and abundant in mercy, forgiving iniquity and transgression; but He by no means clears the guilty, visiting the iniquity of the fathers on the children to the third and fourth generation." Isn't it good to know that we who have our sins covered by the Blood of Jesus have been given the power to break every curse in our family? Because of Calvary we are free and forgiven.

I heard Dave Roever say on TV once that he questioned God when he had surgery and had a colostomy bag. Very angrily, he said to God, "Don't I have enough scars, that you had to give me another one?" He had been severely wounded in Vietnam to the point of parts of his face and body were gone and scarred beyond recognition. He then said, "It's good God doesn't kill stupid." He then said that God spoke to him and said, "Dave, you have scars, but you don't have wounds."

That spoke volumes to me. We must let God heal us, as the enemy of our soul was there during each time we were wounded. If he can keep us wounded, he can cause infections in our spirit that will infect or affect others around us--even our children. I don't want my children and grandchildren to suffer from my suffering, and if I let God heal me, they will learn great lessons of love and truth from me.

We have the authority to be healed. It is our God-given right, but we must take it. You don't want the infection of self-pity to come in, as it speaks volumes to your soul.

You may wonder why I have written so much here about inner healing when we are talking about spiritual warfare. The more healed and delivered your inner person is, the more power over the enemy you will have. Yes, the Blood of Jesus is your power. The enemy cannot come in unless he is invited in by hidden sin and you having little or no strength to fight the temptation of it.

In spiritual warfare that we are getting into, you must realize that the enemy you will be coming against in someone else's life is going to throw everything at you he can, trying to stop you. Give him nothing to war against you with. You do not have to be perfect, but just forgiven and working on the inward man.

SPIRITUAL WARFARE

Ephesians 6:12 "For we do not wrestle against flesh and blood, but against principalities, against powers, against the rulers of the darkness of this age, against spiritual hosts of wickedness in the heavenly places." In my previous chapters, I have shared with you concerning this scripture and what it means to us in depth.

It is very important to take to heart the scripture prior to this one, **Ephesians 6:11** that tells us to "Put on the whole armor of God, that you may be able to stand against the wiles of the devil." Wiles here mean scheming of the devil. That is why I began with inner healing as part of your spiritual strategy. The unhealed wounds and weaknesses we have can fall under and to the schemes of the enemy and render you helpless at the accusations of the devil. One day, I was being bombarded in my inner self about how inadequate I was and guilty of everything. I finally took a stand and yelled, "I know I am not perfect, and that is why I needed a Savior, ok! So go talk to my Father. You will have to walk through the Blood of His Son Jesus to get to Him, because that is where I stand." That day I won a great victory when I agreed with my adversary quickly, yet reminded him of who I am and who I belong to.

You never go into battle unless you are prepared for it. No soldier goes in without training and trusting who backs them up. You have all of Heaven backing you up. Be all you can for the Lord before you go into war. Repent if you feel there is anything you may have said, thought or did that you are feeling guilty of. Guilt will hold you back and will convince you that you have no access to kingdom rights, so repent and forgive your human self for all its flaws and short comings, as we all have them. Like I said in an earlier chapter, Katherine Kuhlman said in one of her books, and I live by these words and share them with everyone--especially those who come to me for counseling. She said, "If I live in all my yesterdays, I will have no tomorrows." Apply that thought to all your fears and doubts, and realize memories can be the enemy's weapon, as he still has access to your mind/intellect.

Circumstances may arise to test your faith and trust in God. Illness may attack your body. Financial crisis may arise, or anything the enemy knows to throw at you. Remember when you are going into spiritual warfare that your enemy is also a warrior and is just as determined to win as you are. Remember he knows he has power, but you not only have the higher power, but you walk in authority over him. Remember the Word, have it in you. **1 John 4:4,** "You are of God, little children, and have overcome them, because He who is in you is greater than he who is in the world."

Fear is one of the enemy's biggest weapons he tries to use against us. Memorize the following scriptures, **1 John 4:18**, "There is no fear in love; but perfect love casts out fear, because fear involves torment. But he who fears has not been made perfect in love." Unconditional love is one of the hardest truths to come into, because in this world we live in conditions and performances that seem to determine and describe who we love and why. God is love, so fear has got to bow the knee.

Isaiah 54:17, "No weapon formed against you shall prosper, And every tongue that rises against you in judgment You shall condemn. This is the heritage of the servants the Lord, And the righteousness from Me, says the Lord." Therefore, the enemy's weapons are not effective, especially if you have been taking care of the carnal man, which is your soul.

Psalms 91 is a chapter to be read daily. Especially the following scriptures. They will be the most amazing and powerful scriptures you will use to encourage yourself in preparation to go into warfare. Get them deep in your heart.

1) He who dwells in the secret place of the Most High shall abide under the shadow of the Almighty.

2) I will say of the Lord, "He is my refuge and my fortress; My God, in Him I will trust."

3) Surely He shall deliver you from the snare of the fowler and from the perilous pestilence.

5) You shall not be afraid of the terror by night, nor the arrow that flies by day.

7) A thousand may fall at your side, and ten thousand at your right hand; but it shall not come near you.

10) No evil shall befall you, nor shall any plague come near your dwelling;

11) For He shall give His angels charge over you, to keep you in all your ways.

14) Because He has set His love upon Me, therefore I will deliver him; I will set him on high, because he has known My name.

15) He shall call upon Me, and I will answer him; I will be with him in trouble; I will deliver him and honor him.

PREPARATIONS FOR SPIRITUAL WARFARE

Fasting and Prayer: In **Matthew 17:19**, the disciples asked Jesus why a demon would not come out of a child when they commanded it to. Jesus said in **verse 20**, "Because of your unbelief; For assuredly, I say to you, if you have faith as a mustard seed, you will say to this mountain move from here to there, and it will move; And nothing will be impossible for you." **Verse 21** "However, this kind does not go out except by **prayer and fasting**."

Fasting and prayer prepares you in getting everything out of your way and getting your mind solely on God and His Word. You are giving Holy Spirit your everything and He is giving you His power for strong faith in Jesus. You need to have fasting for three days, just liquids unless you have health issues. Then do what you feel comfortable with. This is if you are casting out demons in someone who is possessed. Fasting should be done in each of us as Christians on a regular basis; however, when in spiritual warfare it will be a must.

Be very selective with whom you ask to help you. Take time to check their spirit. Test every spirit. **1 John 4:1** "Beloved, do not believe every spirit, but test the spirits, whether they are of God; because many false prophets have gone out into the world." When you see a small "s" in the word "spirit", remember in the Bible, it is speaking of the spirit of man or demonic spirits. The spirit of someone that wants to help you may need more deliverance than the one you are delivering. Some people love chasing demon's because it is their own nature that wants to have and use the power of God and Jesus to make them feel superior. Never forget **Luke 10:19-20**, "Behold, I give you the authority to trample on serpents and scorpions, and over all the power of the enemy, and nothing shall by any means hurt you." Nevertheless do not rejoice in this, that the spirits are subject to you, but rather rejoice because your names are written in Heaven." Back up to verse 18 where Jesus states, "I saw Satan fall like lightning from Heaven." To me, this is one of the scriptures that prove we are in warfare.

Another thing you should do is take Communion. In doing so, it will lift you up out of your kingdom here on earth and help bring you into the kingdom of God and solidify His promises and protection.

You will need to verbally bind up the spirits and their powers. **Matthew 18:18** "Assuredly, I say to you, whatever you bind on earth will be bound in heaven, and whatever you loose on earth will be loosed in heaven." All that I have written are tools you will need. I must tell you that your biggest need other than the Word will be the Presence of the Holy Spirit and His leading. Therefore, here is where tongues come into releasing His power. Be spirit led. If you don't know what to do, stop and pray and praise. Songs that will help you are songs about His Blood that was shed, such as, "The Blood Will Never Lose Its Power," "Oh the Blood of Jesus," and praise songs. Only God can inhabit the praise of His people. That's why there is power in praise. The enemy cannot stand praise and worship.

You will want to anoint yourself and anyone that is helping you with oil. It will unify you with one another and the Spirit. Have a time of prayer with your team.

The above is relating to casting demons out of people. I will attempt to give you some guidelines that have produced the breaking of curses and spells on people and places.

THE CLEANSING OF HOMES AND PROPERTIES

With anointing oil, begin at the highest room reachable to you and begin to anoint windows and doorways, even opening attics and closet doors. Anoint the facings. Do not go overboard with the oil. Just anoint your hands and touch those places spoken of above. Move through the upstairs, speaking the Word and especially say, "No plague can come nigh my dwelling place." Command any evil spirits to go before you as you do this. Then go to the basement and do the same thing, commanding always for them to go before you. Now come up to the main floor and do the same, then command them to the front door and open the door, then command them to leave, in the Name of Jesus. Anoint the threshold and remember to say as you anoint your threshold and repeat that "No plague can come near my dwelling place ever again." That's the promise in **Psalms 91**, remembering that "all His promises are yea and amen." **II Corinthians 1:20.** Be sensible and do not yell out your door or make a spectacle of what you are doing. Your neighbors do not need to know.

As soon as convenient, go to your yard and anoint the four corners of your property. As you anoint your last corner, command the spirits to leave and not return. As you do this, remind the enemy that you have made a Blood line of Jesus around your property and he can never come on it again. Again I say, do not let your neighbors know what you are doing.

If your children or you are having problems with dreams or night terrors, you may want to anoint cloths and pray the Word over them, binding the enemy and loosing the Blood and power of His promises over the cloth. Then place them under your children and spouse's mattresses, for protection and deliverance. I have even anointed beds. Never let them know what you have done. I have anointed chairs, especially in churches, and this has been proven to be very effective. Then release your ministering spirits/warring angels. **Hebrews 1:14** "Are they not all ministering spirits sent forth to minister for those who will inherit salvation?" He is talking about angels here. I used to think and quote that they minister "to" us, then one day I saw that it said "for" us. Call them out to help you.

You may want to put oil on your shoes and walk around your property, or when you are going into someone else's home that you are praying for, you may want to do this and pray as you are driving there.

Praying in tongues is so effective, and it edifies you and puts the enemy in confusion. If you don't have that gift functioning in your experience, then sing praises to God by just telling Him in your own new song, from your heart of love for Him.

Warning: Please do not look for demons or demonic activity in every situation and circumstances, as the enemy can consume you and then you can become oppressed yourself. Be aware, but not a demon chaser. Look only unto God, the Author and Finisher of your salvation. Blessings.

ABOUT THE AUTHOR

Dr. Janelle Wade lived in fear for much of her life, as she struggled with the horror of secret child abuse and incest. Searching for answers and freedom, she would spend five years in witchcraft and bondage, with no hope of getting out. After she received Jesus Christ as an adult, she was delivered from demonic possession, drug addiction, and her painful childhood memories. She travels extensively, telling all who will listen that she is "a captive set free" through the love and power of Jesus Christ. She founded Just Believe Ministries in 1983. She and her husband, Kirk, have ministered on *700 Club*, *TBN*, *TCT*, and many other Christian and secular talk shows. Dr Wade has spoken at many major colleges across the United States. She is used as a conference speaker and in revival meetings, as well as counseling ministry in the office and in the many churches she speaks in. Many have been saved, experienced inner healing and deliverance through her experiential knowledge and her deep love of Jesus Christ and His Word.

63728051R00087

Made in the USA
Lexington, KY
16 May 2017